LEADERSHIP MATTERS

BRINGING OUT THE LEADER WITHIN YOU

Bob Johnson

WESTBOW
PRESS®
A DIVISION OF THOMAS NELSON
& ZONDERVAN

WestBow Press books may be ordered through booksellers or by contacting:

WestBow Press
A Division of Thomas Nelson & Zondervan
1663 Liberty Drive
Bloomington, IN 47403
www.westbowpress.com
844-714-3454

ISBN: 978-1-6642-2578-7 (sc)
ISBN: 978-1-6642-2579-4 (hc)
ISBN: 978-1-6642-2577-0 (e)

Library of Congress Control Number: 2021904372

Print information available on the last page.

WestBow Press rev. date: 03/25/2021

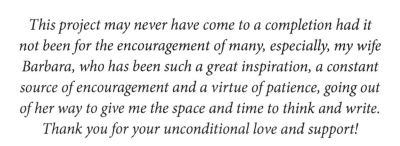

This project may never have come to a completion had it not been for the encouragement of many, especially, my wife Barbara, who has been such a great inspiration, a constant source of encouragement and a virtue of patience, going out of her way to give me the space and time to think and write. Thank you for your unconditional love and support!

And he sat down and called the twelve. And he said to them, "If anyone would be first, he must be last of all and servant of all." —Mark 9:35

CONTENTS

FOREWORD

In every group of people, there is a leader. It may be the one God has called to lead a board, an organization, or a business. It may be a doctor who has donated a significant amount of money to a group. It can be a lady who heads the women's group, or it may be the founder of an organization who strives to perform the task that is at hand. Nonetheless, there are principles of leadership that, when followed, can help a person accomplish what God has directed him or her to do in a manner that is both effective as well as pleasing to Him.

Writing to the Ephesians, the apostle Paul said, "The Holy Spirit has made you overseer" (Acts 20:28). This is the image of a shepherd who leads the flock. A sheep dog nips at the heels of sheep in a flock to motivate them, while a good shepherd gently leads the flock, and the sheep follow him. How an individual leads has much to do with the ultimate success or failure of the group he or she leads. An old proverb says, "An army of sheep led by a lion is more powerful than an army of lions led by a sheep."

Bob Johnson is highly qualified to address the issue of leadership—having served on boards of Christian organizations; having been involved in the business world; and having had years of practical experience in leading his own company as well as observing the qualities in others that result in successful leadership.

In this book, *Leadership Matters*, he weaves together personal experience—tried and tested in the business world—as well as speaks from a Christian worldview that brings the blessing of God. It will enrich your life and provide insights and direction that will make you a better, more effective leader no matter where and who you serve.

—HAROLD J. SALA, PhD
Author and Founder of Guidelines International

PREFACE

Leadership. There are already so many books on leadership. Why another? Even the wisest person who ever lived, King Solomon, writer of Ecclesiastes, said, "There is nothing new under the sun" (Ecclesiastes 1:9). So what could I possibly add to what has already been said or written? In a word, nothing. However, in this book, I am choosing to focus on character, competence, conviction, and courage. These, I believe, are the pillars of ethical leadership. I will also be talking about notable characters who displayed exceptional leadership abilities.

But first, what is a good leader? Usually we can recognize a good leader when we see one in action. We can feel the authenticity of a good leader. We are motivated, influenced, inspired, and impacted by effective and affective leaders. Effective leaders know how to get results. The affective leader, on the other hand, knows how to tap into feelings and emotions. Good leaders are excellent communicators, able to articulate a vision, able to send the message clearly and concisely. They care about the people they serve and are willing to sacrifice for the good of others. Exhibiting integrity, they do what they say. They are aware that leadership is stewardship that is not grounded in pure power but in influence.

Many books on the subject leadership are aimed at those at the top or those who aspire to make it there. Certainly I do not wish to turn away any of these prospective readers. But anybody can actually be a leader. Leadership opportunities are presented to us in various situations and circumstances and in the different seasons of our lives. Many leaders will never gain a formal title such as CEO, president, chairperson, principal, or executive, among others, but they are leaders just the same. If we are aware of these leadership opportunities and make an effort to prepare for them, we can make a larger impact and contribution to the society with our lives. We may not have any foreknowledge of when the call for leadership will present itself, be it a situation or season, but when leadership calls, we need to be prepared. If you are called to step into leadership, embrace it instead of avoiding it.

This book is meant to target those who find themselves looking at leadership at any level, regardless of status or position, hoping to influence, impact, inspire, and encourage. When Providence opens an opportunity to lead, it helps to be prepared for it. When all is said and done, leadership is a choice or, more accurately, a calling. We must continuously learn and grow in order to rise to the occasion and act when leadership calls.

I am expressing my thoughts from a Christian worldview. I do not make apologies for my convictions, what I believe, and how it forms my thinking. I believe in God's sovereignty and the moral truth of the Bible. All of creation and all of life starts and ends with God. Not one of us is here by accident. We were made for a purpose, and leading is one of those purposes. And it all starts with leading ourselves and subordinating ourselves to truth.

I hope that what is written in the following pages will help you and any other leader think about how effective (and affective) leadership can influence, inspire, and impact others for the greater good. Leadership matters, and it's a good time to develop the leader in you.

CHAPTER 1

HOME

Burrowing deeper under the warm covers, I tried to ignore my mother's voice calling me to rise and shine. The room was dark and cold in the early-morning hours, and jumping out of bed was something you had to brace yourself for. The dead of winter in Northern Michigan can be hostile, especially for a twelve-year-old kid being summoned to leave the comfort of a warm bed.

Our home was an old two-story structure built much in the way of an older farmhouse. Located in a little community at the tip of Michigan, our house was heated by a coal furnace that had to be cleaned out of ashes and the accumulated clinkers at least once a week. That meant that the fire had to die during the night, and freezing temperatures outside brought the inside temperature down to very uncomfortable levels. Getting out from under a cotton sheet blanket, a wool blanket, and a heavy but warm handmade quilt was an act of courage. It didn't take long for me to get dressed! I was tasked with cleaning the furnace. It required getting all the ash and clinkers through the grates at the bottom of the furnace, down to the bottom holding area, and then the ashes were shoveled out in buckets that were carried out of the house.

In the meantime, a fire was rekindled to generate heat in the house. It was a tough job for a kid. Why did it have to be me? Well, by this time, my father had passed away eleven years before. He died in an automobile accident when I was a year old. My older brother and sister, in their early twenties, were no longer living at home. My

1

fifteen-year-old sister still living at home had some medical issues and also had other chores more suited for a young girl. So, at twelve, I was the man of the house.

Growing Up in a Single-Parent Home

Growing up in a single-parent home always presents hardships that can ultimately have an impact on a child's character and how he or she views the world. My father died just before Christmas on December 19. Back then, our family was living in Detroit. With the daunting task of raising four children alone, my mother thought it would be easier to relocate to a small town near where she grew up. She packed us up and moved to the small town of Cheboygan, Michigan. Because of the age range among my siblings, my mother faced what could be described as raising two sets of kids, a ten-year span between the oldest and me. I was a late arrival to the family, my mother being forty-one years old when I was born.

Mom never remarried, and her sole mission was to raise us, her four children, and ensure that we all received a high school education. Her own formal education went as far as the eighth grade, but she was intelligent and far from uneducated. She had a good command of the English language while also being able to speak fluent Swedish, and she had a gift of thinking and communicating clearly. Just try to beat her in Scrabble. Nobody could. She instilled the virtues of personal responsibility, respect for those in authority, honesty, and a strong work ethic.

Do Things Right

Household chores were a part of that learned responsibility, and there were right ways and wrong ways of doing them. Shortcuts were not tolerated! A job should be done well, or you did it over. Washing the floor always required two pails of water: a pail for hot, soapy water

2

and a pail for cool, clear water for rinsing, along with a well-wrung-out towel to dry and wipe up any residue. No mops! A clean floor required getting on your hands and knees, applying good old-fashioned elbow grease. One day, I tried to

Shortcuts were not tolerated! A job should be done well, or you did it over.

shortcut this process in my haste to join a pick-up baseball game. No one would notice if I didn't get everything under the table, right? As I headed out the door, Mom called me back to do the entire floor over, one more time from the beginning.

There were many other chores that required meeting my mother's standards. You did what was expected, or you did it over until she was satisfied. So, at the age of twelve, I learned that doing chores was my responsibility and part of the privilege of living at home. I didn't get an allowance in exchange for my hard work. In fact, it was never discussed. My mother had neither the inclination nor the resources to pay an allowance. At an early age, I had to learn that if I wanted something beyond the necessities, I would have to find a way to earn the money for it. Mom told me in no uncertain terms that I needed to understand that the world doesn't owe anybody a living. You have to go out and earn it!

My First Job

One summer, I had the bright idea that I could earn money by cutting the neighbors' grass. So I set out in my neighborhood to find customers. I launched my business the summer I was twelve. Very soon, I learned that mowing was an arduous task using a manual lawn mower. To solve that problem, I made my first capital investment. Drawing on the reputation of my hardworking mother, who accompanied me to our local hardware store, I was able to sell my idea to Mr. Cline, the owner of our J J Post Hardware store. I had to convince Mr. Cline that I could increase profits and improve my business by investing in a power mower. My rationale was, with my added capacity, I could generate revenue between ten and fifteen dollars a week. After I produced a list of existing customers and getting a stern lecture from him about responsibility to settle my liability, we made an agreement to set up an installment plan. With a small down payment of fifteen dollars, I could pay off the remainder in eight weeks. Thus, the Johnson Lawn Patrol was officially launched. Every week, I would show up at the hardware store and hand over five dollars. I actually paid the liability off early, and Mr. Cline did not charge any interest.

The Gift of Spiritual Foundation

My mother taught me many things, but the greatest legacy she passed on to me was a spiritual foundation. Church attendance was mandatory. We attended the Evangelical Covenant Church, and services were held both Sunday morning and evening. In addition, there was the midweek prayer meeting. The evening service was less formal and on occasion was even preached in Swedish to accommodate a large, rural Swedish community on the outskirts of town. Despite the fact that I did not understand Swedish, my attendance was required. It was in those early years that I learned all the Bible stories, memorized scripture, and learned all the Sunday school songs. Mom loved music and played the piano. We would sing together, and because of her influence, I developed a love for music, particularly Christian music. To this day, my memory is saturated with the words of literally hundreds of hymns and gospel songs.

Attendance at church was also required when we had revival services. One time, Rev. Rudy Peterson, an evangelist, stayed at our home for a whole week. He preached with gusto from the pulpit, but he was much quieter at our house. He would spend time in prayer and preparation for the week of services, but one afternoon, he led me through a biblical word study. We used the word *praise*, and we examined several passages in the Bible that discuss when we should praise the Lord, how we should praise Him, where we should praise Him, and why we should praise Him. I still have this lesson outlined in the Bible I used as a kid. After our study, Reverend Rudy invited me

4

to accept Jesus as my personal Lord and Savior. We knelt by the couch in our living room, and I, with all the sincerity and understanding of a young boy, made a decision to follow Jesus. It was the beginning of God's call in my life. Although my spiritual growth languished in my early adult years, it would be rekindled later when I renewed my commitment to place my faith and trust in Jesus Christ. After renewing my commitment to God, I began to grow more spiritually, compared to the first time.

My Mother, My Teacher

Molding and shaping character starts early on in our lives, and it often starts at home. Parents need to lead children by giving them unconditional love, affection, and a sense of security balanced by encouragement, correction, and direction. My mother never talked to me about being a leader, nor did she give any conscious thought to thinking about herself as a leader, but she was. She led by example and by teaching and training. She persevered through many hardships and heartbreaks, and looking back, it is hard for me to comprehend how she survived. Financial resources were scarce. She lost two children, both of my sisters, before she passed away. Mom complained very little through her struggles and lived out her life fully until she died at eighty-six years old. She did little to guide me into the business career that I ultimately chose, but she did much to prepare me for life.

She effectively communicated words of wisdom and practical teaching, and she would drive her messages home at the appropriate time. Aside from teaching me that the world doesn't owe me a living and that I have to go out and earn my way, she also taught me how to conduct myself. When I ventured out with my young pals, she would admonish me, "Let your conscience be your guide." When I made excuses that I couldn't do something because I didn't know how, she would say, "You will never learn any younger," and then promptly engage me and instruct me in what needed to be done. There were a few times in my young life when my rhetoric didn't match up to my actions, and my mother would quickly remind me, "What you do speaks so loudly I can't hear what you say." She would emphasize that words were empty without action. You do what you say. Perhaps my all-time favorite advice, when she warned me to avoid vices like smoking and drinking (which were probably the very worst things a person could do back then), she would tell me, "Bad habits are easy to acquire but long-term hard to live with. Good habits are difficult to acquire but long-term easy to live with."

My mother, whose character was shaped by difficult and challenging times, had a strong work ethic. A competent and a godly woman, she led by the example of self-sacrifice and rock-solid convictions as to what was right and what was wrong and made certain it was communicated to us. She was courageous, stepping up to leading our family after my dad died. She demonstrated a strength that I have identified as the four pillars of good leadership: character, competence, conviction, and courage. Mom's faith was unwavering in difficult situations. Her impact and influence on my life still resonates to this day.

Home Is Where Leaders Are First Forged

Many leaders look back and recognize the importance of their home in shaping them. Ideally, home is where love and support are freely given. Home is where a person is nurtured physically, intellectually, emotionally, and spiritually. People first receive direction, correction, and input where they grow up. In this environment, we learn that there are rules and structure present to develop learning and govern behavior. There is discipline for bad behavior and encouragement for the good. Children first learn to distinguish what is right and what is wrong in the home.

Good parents should identify their children's skills and nurture their potentials without putting them on a pedestal. This will help the kids realize that life does not revolve around one's self and that sometimes sacrifices need to be made for the benefit of others. Home is where we first discover that not all the problems can be solved by mom and dad. Failure can happen, and trying again should be the norm. Social skills are developed and natural talents are honed in the home. In being part of a family, we learn to care about others; to be accountable for our actions; to own our responsibilities; and to give respect.

Why are we best positioned to learn about leadership and self-governance at home? Because it's the launching pad of a potential leader from a developing toddler to a teenager to a young adult. Parents should help make their growing children feel strong, capable, and equipped. Young people turn into responsible and stable adults when they fly out of the nest with a knowledge that they are unconditionally loved. They can say to themselves, "I matter. What I do matters."

> *Parents should help make their growing children feel strong, capable, and equipped.*

Finally, a healthy home environment is where spiritual formation takes root and kids have been led by example and taught biblical teaching. This spiritual foundation will hopefully lead them to make a personal commitment to place their faith and trust in God and become a dedicated follower of Jesus Christ.

I just described to you the ideal home scenario marked by good parental leadership. Parents live out their lives being an example to their children, who watch and learn from what they do. When I am coaching or discipling young men or women, I will sometimes ask them, "Would you like your kids to have a marriage just like yours?" If the answer is no, it is time to make some changes. Something needs to be done to have a stable and healthy home.

But Not All Homes Are Perfect

Many home environments fall short of perfection, some worse than others. Unfortunately, in such cases, parental leadership responsibilities take a back seat to self-interest. As a result, children are neglected. With dual incomes sometimes needed to meet the household expenses, some parents are too tired or too absorbed in their own lives to expend the effort to create a healthy environment for their children. Oh, they might live in an upscale neighborhood and lavish their kids with every conceivable luxury—giving them the latest in entertainment, fashion, and technology. After all, they want their kids to have fun and enjoy their youth. These parents try to give their kids the best, better than what the parents had when they were young. They shield their kids from the reality that life in a broken world sometimes means experiencing difficult challenges, disappointment, and pain.

Some parents also act as their kids' friends and solve all their problems. As a consequence, the kids become spoiled, having an entitlement mentality. They grow up with unrealistic expectations about life and will be in for a rude awakening when they become adults who can't always get what they want.

And then there are homes where families struggle to survive with meager resources. Illnesses and other hardships can impose difficulties that require a child to take on responsibilities that interfere with her education and social development. (Yet, in many cases, poverty-stricken kids grow up and succeed through sheer hard work and grit. Hardships can and do develop character, where, on the other hand, ease of life does nothing more than give a person a false sense of entitlement.)

Finally, there are home situations that can be described as dysfunctional and toxic. More and more children are born out of wedlock. Marriages are breaking apart at alarming rates, and more and more kids are being raised by an overtaxed single parent. Most often, it is a single mom who has to act as both mother and father. Kids miss having a male role model to dire consequences. So if the leadership of one or both parents is not present in the home, kids will often act out in self-destructive ways.

Many teens and young adults go around carrying heavy emotional baggage as a result of being a part of dysfunctional homes. They fail to take on the responsibilities of life after graduation from high school (if they graduate) and are ill-prepared to meet the demands of adult life. Of those who struggle, some will eventually learn how to survive on their own. As for the others, these young adults will return home and depend on their parents or, worse, turn to the dark side of our society and end up on the streets.

When these young, undisciplined, or unprepared adults enter into the workforce, their bosses are then tasked with trying to fix the effects of bad parenting. The fact that many young adults are not equipped to face the real world is handicapping our society and culture. We are so lacking for leadership skills everywhere—in the home, businesses, schools, even our churches and in our government. (The latter wanting to promise everything but deliver programs that further erode self-reliance and personal responsibility.)

The home is the first place where leadership is modeled and learned. As we've looked at different aspects of home environment, and while there is much concern about how families are failing and falling short of providing a healthy environment, there are still many young people who give us hope. Whether they come from good, solid, or disadvantaged homes, they want to grow, learn, make a difference, and live meaningful and purposeful lives. Those in leadership positions must encourage their growth and development and help them flourish.

Many people have had this kind of influence in my life. Although my mother wasn't the only person who helped shape my character and convictions, she holds the distinction of having made the most significant impact. Parents, your leadership role as a parent is not a choice. The moment you became a parent, you were called to lead!

> *The fact that many young adults are not equipped to face the real world is handicapping our society and culture.*

Growing Up by Taking Responsibility

Let me tell you about Mike. He left Vietnam just before the communists took over. His parents stayed behind and sent him, along

9

with eight brothers and sisters, to America. The plan was that as each sibling reached the age of eighteen, he or she would be responsible for taking care of the younger siblings. So when Mike turned eighteen, he took over from one of his older siblings and took care of his two younger sisters. He worked an entry-level job and provided food and housing for the three of them. They lived simply and had to make some sacrifices, but they made it. It was a big responsibility to take on at such a young age, but it shaped his character, and today he is an expert in his industry. Eager to improve himself, he is contemplating going back to college to further his formal education. Although Mike is a couple decades younger than me, he displays incredible maturity after going through struggles, doing hard work, and by taking responsibility.

Many parents in our country today try to protect their children from experiencing hardships by not giving them any big responsibilities. Their children are too wrapped up in playing video games and engaging in social media instead of reading books and developing face-to-face relationships. As a result, these young people are ill-prepared to face the demands of life. They fail in their commitments—to a purpose and in their relationships. If the future is dependent on leadership, there is reason to be concerned about what lies ahead for future generations. While there are young families who are working hard to counter the negative forces of our culture, there are still many who neglect to provide good parental leadership. Statistics don't lie. Pew Research Center reports that the US has the world's highest rate of children living in single-parent homes. Nearly 25 percent of our children in this country live with one parent. More and more families are breaking up. Something needs to change, but where does one start? What can we do to make a difference in our society today? We'll address this later in the book.

CHAPTER 2

DO YOU HAVE WHAT IT TAKES TO LEAD?

Steve, a manager in his late twenties, found himself in a precarious position. His boss, Art, had just been fired for embezzlement. After doing an extensive investigation, the higher-ups realized that Art didn't act alone. The crime took place in a large distribution center housing high-value products. The people involved in the embezzlement were all rounded up while the remaining members of the management team were required to take a lie detector test. Steve was one of the first to be tested. With his heart pounding hard after being wired, he tried his best to calm himself. But this thought still lingered in his head: *What if they think I'm guilty?* He felt the same tension like everyone else who went through the process. As the investigation continued, more people were taken out. Many speculated that the entire management team, even though they were innocent, would be terminated.

Becoming a Leader

Several days after doing the polygraph test, Steve was called to the front office. He walked into the senior executive's office full of anxiety and trepidation. He was anxious, yes, but he knew in his heart that he was not involved in any way. He had zero knowledge of the embezzlement while it was going on. Much to his surprise, he was offered to assume the position left by his former boss. It was a huge step up in responsibility.

He accepted the job, filled with excitement and relief, but at the same time, he also felt apprehension and fear. He wasn't fully prepared, but nevertheless, top management believed that he would grow into the job. They promised to give him support and encouragement, and he was teamed up with a mentor, who later became his lifelong friend. While senior leadership acknowledged that this promotion would be a big challenge to Steve, they believed he could succeed based on his past performance. (Steve learned later on that he was only one of two managers who passed the polygraph test.)

Steve was honest with himself and knew that this new role would stretch him. This was a division of a large national company, and now he would run the second-largest distribution center in the system. He knew he had to display confidence and earn the trust of his subordinates, in addition to the people in management who believed in him. Fortunately for Steve, his former boss had a very capable and knowledgeable administrative assistant, Johnnie, who had vast experience and actually knew more about the operation than did Steve. They quickly bonded, partly because Steve admitted that he didn't know everything and humbly asked for Johnnie's help and support. Steve jumped into the new role despite his lack of skill and experience. He didn't know much, but he knew enough to know about what needed to be done. With the help of Johnnie and the support of others, including his mentor, he made some difficult decisions. He selected and promoted new personnel in various leadership positions. As expected, he had to face challenges, particularly around personnel issues. But as he embraced his leadership position, he grew in confidence and competence. For Steve, this huge jump in his position launched the beginning of a successful career that ultimately landed him a top spot in the company.

What Steve Did Right

In a nutshell, here is a list of what Steve did to tackle the unexpected challenge in his career:

> He approached the assignment soberly, acknowledging that he didn't know everything. In fact, looking back now, he admits that he wasn't sure about what he thought he knew.
>
> He had an attitude of a learner and was open to learn from everyone, including those who now worked for him.
>
> He worked tirelessly to get to know his new team members. He realized he would not achieve results on his own. He won over the employees and listened to them and worked hard to gain credibility and their trust.
>
> He realized that courage comes from working through his fear. He took action that aligned with what he communicated even when he knew there would be pushback.

How about you? What will you do when you are suddenly thrust into leadership like Steve? Are you a young person who is tasting independence for the first time and wondering where to begin? Do you have what it takes to lead? If not, how will you get there? Consider doing the following things to be a great leader:

Be trustworthy. Most people start at the bottom and begin their vocational journey from there. This might be the case for you too. There is a difference between experiential learning and content learning. You leverage your education—your content learning—to application. Whatever you learned in textbooks and in the classroom, you are now putting into practice. Things you say and do have real-life consequences. People don't always behave in ways you might expect. There might be conflicts. There *will* be conflicts! You are now in the arena where theory and practice do not always line up neatly. You continue to build on your knowledge base and polish your skills to apply your knowledge effectively in order to make a measurable and meaningful contribution to the company. You have to prove yourself to others—that is, prove that you can get something done and work with other people. You take the initiative, learn, and gain experience and the trust of others. You work hard and follow through and show that you are dependable and responsible, able to deliver excellent results.

From the very beginning, everything starts with trust. Earning the trust of your boss as well as those who work with you is key to your success. Earning trust, learning your role, accepting responsibility, and gaining competence lead to eventually getting opportunities for promotion. Keeping that trust is the key to staying in leadership, even at the lowest level of leadership. Building trust never ends. In fact, the need for it only escalates as you assume higher leadership roles. Trust is foundational for all relationships and is established over time by demonstrating that you do what you say and you say what you do. It takes time to build trust, but be warned: your trust can be lost very quickly by not doing what you say you will do. To repeat what my mother used to say, "What you do speaks so loudly I can't hear what you say." In any leadership position, in any lasting relationship, everything starts with trust.

Be competent. Competent people can be trusted. Look for challenges and opportunities to take on more than is expected in order to build competence and knowledge. If we actively look, there are challenges and opportunities all around us. Develop a curious mindset about the people you serve and the processes used in the work in which you are engaged. Proactively challenge yourself to look for problems to solve and focus on processes and systems that are in place. Does something need to be improved? Then work on solutions. Leadership requires courage. When you do step out, you might experience uncertainty and doubt. This is normal. Many successful people who exhibit courage and take on difficult problems look back and recount how stepping out and exploring a new territory where they had to persevere always brought out their best in their drive to succeed. Don't fall into a victim mentality when your progress seems stymied. Learn to know when to persevere and when to acknowledge and admit when you're wrong. Humility and transparency also build trust. Don't blame others when something goes wrong that is of your own doing.

Be courageous. Ask questions without fear. So many times, we are reluctant to speak up and ask questions or offer input. Put yourself in these situations where you are challenged to grow. With time, experience, and practice, you will gain skills and accumulate working knowledge of what it takes to be competent in your role, and you set yourself up to lead. This effort should never cease. Then it is a matter of stepping out and leading in the pursuit of a vision, an idea, a cause that inspires, or a problem that needs to be solved, which is eventually realized by taking action. In short, we ultimately learn to lead through practice.

Believe in yourself. Listen and watch. Learn. If you don't believe in yourself, you can't effectively lead others. Be authentic. Don't try to be somebody you are not. Work on always being in the moment and being self-aware. Know the trigger points that activate your negative emotions and learn how to manage them and keep them under control. Self-control is the key to self-mastery and learning to lead. Learn to lead yourself before leading others.

Be willing to grow. Leadership and personal growth begin on the inside when you become aware of your strength and weaknesses. It is your responsibility to purposefully and intentionally develop your skills. Your professional development is your responsibility and cannot be the responsibility of someone else. Other people may help you, but in the end, you have to take responsibility for your personal and professional growth. Make an honest assessment of who you are and what you want. Clarify your values and convictions. This requires thought and introspection. We all have strengths and weaknesses, and while it is obvious to lead with strengths, you can't ignore weakness. Know your weaknesses, manage them, and always work toward polishing your skills.

Be excited about your work. You have to love what you do. If you don't love what you do, then you have to find a way to love what you do. If you can't do this, leave your job and find something else. Of course, I'm not saying that you are going to love every aspect of what you do, because that would be unrealistic. We will always have duties and responsibilities related to our work that are not fun. I'm talking about the larger context of what you do. I have never had a job that I didn't enjoy. I always found a way, even as a blue-collar worker in a warehouse, to enjoy my work.

Nothing is permanent, and we live in a constantly changing world, and you have to change with it. Whatever you are doing today will not last. Consider what you are doing now as preparation for what comes next. Embrace change when it comes. Whatever you learn as an individual and as a leader will benefit you for the rest of your life.

Are You Truly a Leader?

Some may view themselves as leaders, but in truth, they are not. These are the people who have merely gained leadership positions as a by-product of personality, popularity, status, or politics, or perhaps by family connection (i.e., born into the inheritance of a family business). The point is someone may be thrust into leadership by being granted a title, but that does not make one a leader. True leaders are those who have purposefully and intentionally worked to shape their character to gain trust. Committed to learning, they are constantly building competence by accumulating knowledge, developing skills, and getting things done. Leaders live by their convictions and willingly display their courage by making hard choices. They take risks and do difficult things.

There are many good and effective leaders without formal titles. In fact, when boiled down to its essence, a good definition of a leader could be those who picture where they are going and engage and inspire others to commit to take action. Leaders are people who live their daily lives unselfishly, exemplifying good character and courage. These leaders go out of their way to help others become better at making their unique contribution to the task and even care about what happens to their people outside work. There are many who act as good leaders and yet aren't even aware of the contribution they make.

Lisa is such a person. Her coworkers gravitate to her, seeking her counsel and advice about business problems or personal issues. Always positive and upbeat, she goes out of her way to make new hires feel part of the team. She is a big influence in promoting the culture and performance standards of the company. When asked if she would like to lead and manage the team, she would firmly say, "No, thank you." But nevertheless, whether she believes it or not, Lisa is a leader who makes a big contribution to the success of the team.

Good Leaders and Bad Leaders

There is the saying that leaders are born and not made. There are those who seem to be gifted with a natural DNA of talent and personality where it seems obvious that this person should lead. They seem to be natural born leaders who always take charge. But regardless of DNA, talents, or personality, leadership skills can be learned and developed by intentional learning and purposeful practice. Potential leaders come from all walks of life and, many times, make an impact for better or sometimes, unfortunately, for worse. The fact is that there are good leaders and bad leaders. In my experience, I have had it both ways.

One CEO I enjoyed working with headed a new acquisition. What takes place many times in an acquisition, especially a company with a history of poor results, is the turnover of some or all members of the management team. In this case, the field management stayed in place, and majority of the corporate management members were asked to leave. Since I was hired to be part of the corporate team, I watched and learned how this leader built trust and established credibility. First, the CEO invested time getting to know everyone on the team.

Displaying transparency, he introduced himself and told them about his expectations. He discussed roles and responsibilities and painted a picture of how we would work together to create something special. To establish rapport among team members, he created opportunities for socializing. From the very beginning, he worked hard toward building a culture of trust and openness. In particular, he emphasized that "everything was new for the first time." He did not want surprises. He didn't want to know about lingering and ongoing problems after the fact. Constantly he would communicate his vision for the future and what we could accomplish together. We worked on establishing teams at every level of the organization and taught the purpose of teamwork and established norms of how we would conduct ourselves. He emphasized not just customer service but customer satisfaction.

At every level of the organization, teams were formed, and each team established its own purpose. During meetings, robust discussions were encouraged. Bosses didn't simply dispense edicts from the top. Decisions were made, ideas were birthed, initiatives were taken, accountability was established, and timelines were clarified. Senior management modeled and promoted team development. High-performance teams were talked about—how they looked, performed, and held one another accountable. It started with the senior management team, and it was modeled to every level of the organization. Teams were established to communicate, solve problems, assign accountability, and focus on results. In one year, profits increased tenfold!

Contrast this CEO's leadership style with one of the worst leaders I worked with. He was a well-educated but foul-mouthed individual who led by intimidation. Lording over his people with an inflated ego, he was a self-promoter and a poor role model. He would cast blame on those around him when things went wrong. However, in the business world, he might be regarded as successful because the company grew and was profitable, or at least during the time

> *Teams were established to communicate, solve problems, assign accountability, and focus on results. In one year, profits increased tenfold!*

I was there. I left the company after enduring three years under his leadership. It's true what has been said, "People leave bosses, not companies."

There are good leaders, and there are bad leaders. Both influence and impact others. Outside of the workplace, there are the other leaders, like my mother, who had little professional training but was grounded with strong moral character, competence raising a family, solid convictions of right and wrong, and courage to step out in dire circumstances. She did well in preparing me for life. Now, speaking of life, did you know that we are being shaped to become great leaders in the different seasons of our lives?

CHAPTER 3

SEASONS OF LIFE

The older we get, the more we realize how quickly time passes. Ever noticed how when we were young, waiting a week seemed like a long time, and the next year, an eternity away? Even the psalmist has something to say in Psalm 90:10, 12, "The years of our life are seventy, or even by reason of strength eighty; yet their span is but toil and trouble; they are soon gone, and we fly away. So teach us to number our days that we may get a heart of wisdom." As we mature and get older, we learn that life is short. Let's look at the different seasons of life and how we grow during each stage.

Discovering Who We Are

The first season roughly spans from birth to twenty years old. During this stage, many changes are happening concurrently. We begin life, hopefully, in the security of a stable family. In this environment, we develop and grow physically, mentally, emotionally, and spiritually. Even at a young age, social and personality tendencies will begin to emerge. Shy? Outgoing? Infants give hints, through their behavior, about what kind of people they will grow up to be. As we consider the first twenty years, tendencies become more fixed, and we also see natural talent and giftedness show. During these years, in addition to physical maturation, the mind, spirit, and heart are being shaped. This fact underscores why the leadership of parents is crucial to a child's development during these formative years.

Learning Independence

The second season of life is marked by independence. As a person finishes secondary education, he or she might choose to go to college or find a job, or serve in the military, among the most common options. Usually, people get married and start a family in their twenties. This time period requires an enormous amount of energy, and the learning that takes place is primarily linked to life experience. Theory turns into practice. We begin to learn the distinction between "what we know and what we *really* know," as my wife, Barbara, often says. While we're building a career and managing our finances, we are also working toward having a strong marriage and raising well-adjusted kids who are grounded with a sense of responsibility and purpose. These years can be trying because we're vulnerable to being tired and burned out. This second season, we are bringing a new generation into the world, in a sense dealing with the here and now with a vision of the there and then. If parents in this season of life are not leading well, things can get off track quickly, and their lives and those around them can spiral downward.

During this season, what we have learned from the leadership of our parents can make a huge difference in shaping our future. Sooner or later, we will discover that getting married and having children requires leadership big-time. As the second-generation parents move further into this season of life, time picks up speed. The children grow up faster than their parents can imagine and become adolescents at the cusp of starting out on their own. Then suddenly, or so it seems, the children become adults, and the cycle repeats itself.

Enjoying the Greatest Productivity

For the third season, many people will find themselves as parents of adult children. At this time, the demands of responsibilities around marriage, vocation, and family are established to a degree. However, our world is changing at a faster rate than ever before. We might find that the values and beliefs we tried to instill as our children were growing up are muted by our culture. When this happens (and it will), the leadership role for our now-adult children is even more daunting. This is where good leadership in the family pays off. Family leadership (of mom and dad) is the most important and lasting influence in how the second generation makes its mark in the society. We'll talk later about our culture, but it's crucial to be a part of a close family and a good church family where the Word of God is taught.

In this season, we could be at the peak of our careers, enjoying our greatest productivity as evidenced by the accomplishment of many life goals. Chances are that many people are relating to their now-grown children and perhaps even grandchildren. We are engaged but have transitioned to a point where our children are independent and self-sufficient. We watch our children from the sidelines as they blaze their own path, lead their own families, and take up leadership positions in their chosen vocation. People in this season of life would ideally have more free time that can be invested in learning, playing a new role in family leadership, and mentoring the next generation. What do we do with the knowledge and skills we have acquired through the years? We can use it to help shape the community where we live, our church, or nonprofit institutions, for good. Depending on where we are financially or positionally, we can invest our time and talent to a whole new track. Or as my friend, mentor/coach Bob Shank says, we're moving from "what you're paid to do to what you're made to do." Bob has committed to help people do just that with the Master's Program. Any Christian businessman should look at this program.

Redeeming Our Past

Admittedly, I have painted the perfect picture, the most ideal scenario of parents producing the next generation of well-prepared leaders. But it could be that the first two seasons of a person's life have been marked by difficult circumstances, pain, and hardships beyond his or her control. There are those who suffer through broken family relationships, divorce, disappointments in career, health problems, or experiencing the consequences of poor decisions. Although we cannot alter our past, we can learn from our mistakes and work toward changing for the better. Much of our character has been shaped by this time, but transformation is still possible. With God's love, forgiveness, and redemptive grace, anything is possible. Will our past cause us to be helpless and hopeless, or will it strengthen us and give us hope? This is where faith in God can transform us like nothing else. The apostle Paul admonishes us, "Do not be conformed to this world, but be transformed by the renewal of your mind, that by testing you may discern, what is the will of God, what is good and acceptable and perfect" (Romans 12:2).

> *Although we cannot alter our past, we can learn from our mistakes and work toward changing for the better.*

While this season of life can be demanding, if we have lived our life well, we will be in the position to finish well. As some of the financial responsibilities have eased, we can slow down and look ahead to think about what we may do that will have a lasting or, even better, eternal impact.

Leaving a Lasting Legacy

Finally, the fourth season of life—barring infirmities—can be a time of excitement and service and can open the potential to create a lasting legacy. This is the time to take risks in terms of investing our time, talent, and resources, without necessarily expecting a financial return. By risks, I don't mean foolish risks. What I'm saying is a person can step out of his or her career focus and bring meaning and purpose beyond work life to finish strong. Ultimately, we are here for one purpose: to bring honor and glory to God.

As we age, we might be focused on self-preservation. It is natural to be cautious and careful. But in this season, if we are too cautious, we can be robbed of joy and satisfaction. If we turn inward and become more and more self-absorbed, worried about health and finances, we face the danger of falling into depression. Some lose their identity associated with life's work and don't know what to do with their free time. Many feel that their children have drifted away, or perhaps they have lost a spouse, and loneliness has set in. Pain, suffering, and loss in this last season of life may be present, but we can still serve the Master by serving others.

If we are in good health during this season of life, we can be productive in ways like never before. We can turn our focus to eternal things rather than the temporal. If we are so blessed, our time, talent, and treasure can be invested in our family, our service, or in any ministry that can advance the Gospel and ease the condition of the less fortunate. To use a sports analogy, the fourth quarter is when players realize that they only have a finite amount of time left in the game. Time is running out, so their every move matters. If you are in this last season of life, this is the time to solidify your legacy. But you may be wondering, *How do I do that?*

It will be wise for us to learn from the example of many admirable leaders. In the next chapter, let's look at the life and legacy of a major Bible character.

CHAPTER 4

LESSONS FROM THE LIFE OF JOSHUA

There are many great stories that can be told about a leader's formation. Many a leader is shaped early on by what happens through his life experience, especially difficult times. Our lives are not made to be lived in isolation. We need the influence of others—family, friends, peers, and mentors. Of the many stories I could choose, one that stands out to me is the story of Joshua in the Old Testament of the Bible.

The Backdrop of His Life

While nothing is written about Joshua's growing-up years, we know something about what was going on around him. The nation of Israel was held captive by the Egyptians, and its people were treated as slaves. The early life of Joshua must have been difficult. The Egyptians were harsh task masters. The Old Testament account tells us that these slave drivers were cruel slave drivers to the Israelites, which resulted in their hardship and suffering. So as Joshua experienced the sad reality of being under Egyptian rule, his character was being molded. It could have made him bitter forever, but instead it made him better. Learning to persevere through difficult times shapes character. The result could have been demoralizing, but not for Joshua. Many great leaders in history were shaped by hardships and painful circumstances. Much of our character is shaped in our formative years (although frankly, it won't feel like leadership training at that time), and Joshua was no exception. This is not to say we have to experience the intense suffering of Joshua, but the fact is that the scars born out of suffering strengthen our character and mature us in many ways that living a life of relative ease and comfort cannot. Character is the bedrock of leadership. Our life experiences and circumstances and how we respond play a big role in shaping our character, and so does the presence of some people in our lives.

Meet Moses, the Mentor

Moses played a big role in developing Joshua as a leader. During his tenure of being under Moses, Joshua learned to serve as a faithful and loyal subordinate. As the mentor-mentee relationship matured, the trust level grew between Moses and his protege at the same time. After the Israelites were finally delivered from Egyptian rule, Joshua continued his character leadership development. When the Israelites wandered through the wilderness, Joshua saw Moses deal with the constant grumbling and complaining of the people.

Ready to Lead

Leadership requires preparation. You cannot take on the mantle of leadership without getting ready for it. Many times, especially when we are young, we get impatient and want to move forward before we're ready. Joshua had to wait forty years before entering the Promised Land, and while he waited, God was preparing him for the biggest leadership challenge of his life. We first learn about Joshua in Exodus, when he was a commander of the Israelites in the battle against the Amalekites. Joshua, the son of Nun, was an assistant to Moses from his youth (see Numbers 11:28).

When Moses died, the responsibility of leading Israel was passed on to Joshua. Joshua undoubtedly learned a great deal from Moses and was prepared by his mentor, along with the experience gained through trials and hardship of being under the Egyptians. Joshua led in handling some of the conflicts the Israelites faced while wandering in the desert for forty years. Because he was prepared, when he was finally tasked to lead the Israelites, his competence and confidence continued to grow.

A True Visionary

One mark of a good leader is competence in many areas but especially around communication, strategic thinking, planning, and execution. Joshua communicated effectively and inspired the Israelites with a God-given vision and inspired a hope for the future. With a clear vision, he led the nation over the Jordan River and into the Promised Land. In Proverbs 29:18 (KJV), we read, "Where there is no vision the people perish." Leaders like Joshua who are leading on a large scale must cultivate the skill and capability to create strategy and vision. Leaders must effectively communicate their planned course of action. Those who are thrust into new leadership positions know that expectations build quickly. Leading an entire nation of people who were many times wayward, Joshua had a huge task of communicating the vision of God's promise to Israel. So, filled with the hope and the promise of a new land flowing with milk and honey, Joshua boldly led them over the Jordan River into a new land. But, as often happens when leaders take on a bold initiative, they encountered some problems. The new land was a land filled with hostile opposition. Joshua, however, was undeterred. With courage and faith, Joshua inspired the multitude of people to move forward. The patience and endurance he learned by going through difficult times prepared him for the huge task ahead. He did it by acting in faith and decisiveness, communicating effectively to inspire a nation of people who seemed always ready to give up when times were tough.

Out of His Comfort Zone and into the Battle

Leadership skills and principles can be taught. But to really know what it means to lead is learned on the job. Leadership books and seminars can teach about leadership, but what really develops the skills and abilities of a leader is being on the battlefield of life. It was during the difficult times that Joshua's character was forged. The real test of character comes when you are taken out of your comfort zone and must step out with courage, competence, conviction, and faith to step up and step into leadership.

God, through Moses, told Joshua to be courageous. In Joshua 1:6 (NIV), we read, "Be strong and courageous, because you will lead these people to inherit the land I swore to their ancestors to give them." Now it was time to put his faith to the test. Would he lead courageously based on his deep convictions? Would he pass the test? The answer was clearly seen as he followed God's leading in a most unusual battle plan of marching around the city of Jericho for seven days, culminating in the blowing of horns and the tumbling down of walls. While we probably won't be called on to lead a nation into battle, it's important to remember that good leadership is about developing the kind of character that holds up under the demands of exercising competence, taking risks, springing into action, and displaying moral courage. Joshua's story proves that if we are reluctant to put to the test what we believe into what we do, we will not accomplish much as a leader.

Building a Strategy

The conquest of the Promised Land required strategic thinking and planning. Again, Joshua's preparation and previous battles had positioned him to lead and think clearly. The first battle for the city of Jericho was followed by a second battle for the city of Ai. In this second battle, Joshua learned a costly lesson. Overconfident, he listened to poor counsel and was complacent in sizing up the strength of his foe (see Joshua 7:3–5). The first attempt to capture Ai resulted in disaster. His advisers thought foolishly and overlooked deceitfulness among the troops. After being defeated by the men of Ai, Joshua stopped and sought counsel from God and corrected the problem. With God's help, Joshua executed a different strategy. The Israelites brought down the city of Ai by using a more conventional battle plan than the one used at Jericho. You can read the battle of Ai yourself in the book of Joshua 7–8.

The result of capturing these two key cities of Jericho and Ai divided the North from the South. Joshua's army had secured strategic routes and cut off key supply routes. Moving quickly and courageously, Joshua responded with decisive action to the south. Seizing an opportunity to surprise the enemies that had marshaled together in the South, Joshua's army marched all night to catch the enemy off guard and quickly overpowered them. With the South beaten, Israel was now positioned to take on the North and fully enter into the Promised Land.

Learning from His Mistakes

Joshua made mistakes but learned from his experiences, both good and bad, and kept on going. Making mistakes is a part of life, but instead of dwelling on them, Joshua used the lessons from the past to learn and grow as a leader. He was quick to acknowledge mistakes and ask for forgiveness, and he sought direction to move forward. With his heart and mind, Joshua led the people. His leadership was strengthened by a well-formed character that was gained by taking courageous action, constant learning and growing, and exercising his faith. Joshua led and followed through, executing the mission. His strategy was clearly thought out and planned and executed with competence and courage, supported by a faith and a belief that his action was accomplished through him but was ultimately directed by God.

Joshua's Legacy

Joshua's focus was on obedience to God. His obedience was cultivated by belief that he put into practice. He led others with his God-given authority but didn't use his position to inflate his ego. Instead, he used his authority to build trust so that he could influence and inspire people. Trust is key and foundational to leadership in the building of relationships. They trusted his leadership. This explains why the tired soldiers willingly marched all night to surprise the enemies in the South and engage in the fight with the enemy and won.

Later in the closing chapter of Joshua's life, he expresses perhaps the best summary of all his priorities and his legacy. Joshua firmly declared in Joshua 24:15, "But as for me and my house we will serve the LORD." There are four key things we can learn from Joshua's life: 1) His character was forged by tests and trials throughout his life; 2) his convictions were anchored to the nonnegotiable values, believing the truth of God's commandments that guided his priorities as a servant leader; 3) his competence was gained by learning from the teaching of his mentor, Moses, and from his own experience; and 4) his courage was displayed when, by faith, he acted decisively in the face of fear.

Leaders like Joshua who are leading on a large scale must cultivate the skill and capability to create strategy and vision.

Joshua left behind an amazing legacy that we still read about today, thousands of years after his death. He did this by leading a nation through many difficult challenges. The question is this: can we, like him, step up to the plate when called upon to lead? Who—or what—are the enemies we are called to defeat?

CHAPTER 5

CHALLENGING THE CULTURE

In our world today—or at least in many Western countries—we don't suffer the same kind of oppression that Joshua and the rest of the Israelites experienced under the Egyptian rule. But although we are not wandering in the desert like they once did, we could make the case that we do face similar desert wanderings. Our culture, like those of the Israelites on their way to the Promised Land, is subject to chaos, rebellion, and groupthink. The leaders of our country, especially those who desire to be godly servant leaders, face daunting challenges. Let's pause and explore the current cultural landscape and how we can lead amidst the challenges.

Overworked Parents and Neglected Children

Good parents want their children to have a better life than what they themselves experienced growing up. Speaking as a parent, we want them to have what their friends have. At least, on the surface, that is what it looks like. Unfortunately, this can have a negative effect. We pursue a comfortable, if not affluent, lifestyle, to the detriment of our children's character. If we don't direct them to righteous living at an early age, they will miss out on the moral virtues that they could have learned by correction. In many cases, the task of training and discipline is outsourced to the schoolteachers while both parents work. Is it any wonder why our leaders are promoting government-sponsored day care? While the motivation may be well intentioned, to relieve parents of their duties in leading and shaping their children will be, in the long term, a disaster.

Many parents struggle to keep a work-life balance—managing their careers and taking care of their children. Sadly, they don't always succeed. Tired from spending the whole day (or week) at work, these parents ignore their children and offer alternatives, like electronics, to keep the kids busy. What happens to the time that parent and child should spend together to talk and have teachable moments? Lost. It's about time people realize that paying attention to our children is more important than giving them what we think they need but actually don't.

The Problem with School

What kind of influence do most schools have on our kids? Not always positive. For instance, they might get integrated into schools that are advocating worldly values. Later on, we wonder why our kids are not learning the basic moral values we were taught. They turn into teens indoctrinated with thinking and beliefs that are far off course from our own. Some schools teach about gender neutrality, saying that gender is a choice. Another controversial topic is the threat of global warming, alarming our young people that the world may cease to exist in a few years. We also coddle our young people to the point that they have become hypersensitive and now require safe places to function.

Because of social pressure, they start believing that they are entitled to everything. Furthermore, our children are not encouraged to think for themselves in the context of understanding the value of truth, honesty, trust, self-reliance, self-sacrifice, self-control, patience, frugality, and hard work. In most cases, our schools are teaching our children *what* to think but not *how* to think. They are basically being brainwashed to think that the world revolves around them and their personal happiness. They hear these messages: *Do whatever makes you happy. Follow your passion.* It's sad to think that there are parents who, instead of guiding their children, let them do whatever they want and allow them to make major decisions for themselves. Should we then be surprised when kids get off track and fail to become responsible adults?

> *They are basically being brainwashed to think that the world revolves around them and their personal happiness.*

Taming Teenagers

Did you know that more and more teachers today are quitting out of fear of repercussions from disciplining students? Many teenagers lack respect for adults. They use foul language, love to argue, and display a total lack of manners. Things are getting so bad now that teachers are afraid of getting attacked by their students in the classroom. These unruly high school students then move on to college, where there is even less restraint against bad behavior. A graduating high school student who visited an elite university came home with stories about cocaine use and wild parties happening at the campus. During spring break, things can get even wilder. These scenarios give us a glimpse of some of the kind of people who will shape the norms of our culture. If we don't address this kind of questionable behavior among the young people, what will our future as a society look like?

Technology

Technology is advancing at an astounding rate. The stimuli in the twenty-first century can be overwhelming! In the age of digital media, one can use many devices—tablets, smartphones, laptops—to consume data. You can even use your watch to take calls or read text messages. Social networks have made it possible to stay connected with apps like Facebook, Twitter, Instagram, and Linked-In. It has become so easy to talk to another person from anywhere in the world. But are we really making meaningful connections?

Studies show the negative effects our advancement in digital technology is having on our kids. More and more people are being diagnosed with ADHD (attention deficit hyperactivity disorder). Usually ADHD is diagnosed in early childhood, but older kids so consumed with gaming and social media are losing the ability to relate to people face-to-face. Parents, who are busy with other tasks, give them smartphones and tablets to keep them occupied. Notice this the next time you are in a restaurant. You'll see people sitting at the table with their heads buried in their smartphones, not talking to each other. Thomas Kersting, in his groundbreaking book *Disconnected: How to Reconnect Our Digitally Distracted Kids*, said this:

> A December 2015 study in the Journal of Clinical Psychiatry found that ADHD diagnoses soared 43 percent in the United in the first decade of this century, with more than one in ten youths now diagnosed with this disorder. The number of teenagers diagnosed with ADHD rose 52 percent between 2003 and 2015. And while ADHD is traditionally more common in boys than girls, the study also found a 55-percent increase in girls being diagnosed with the disorder. The study was not designed to look for the underlying reasons for the changes, but it referred to past studies, suggesting that the rise may be attributed to special-education policy or increased public awareness, which I disagree with. I believe the increase in ADHD diagnoses has everything to do with the amount of time children are spending in front of screens.

Parents need to do something to arrest the damage of digital addiction on children. They must exercise their leadership responsibilities in restricting and controlling the use of technology with their kids.

The Disintegration of Families

Forty percent of children are now living in households with unmarried parents. Living together has gotten so prevalent in our society that people don't give it a second thought. Statistics bear out that even if a couple decides to get married after living together, the divorce rate among those couples who live together before marriage is much higher than for those who marry and then live together! In addition, couples who live together before marriage tend to be less satisfied with their marriages. The US Census Bureau says that the number of couples in cohabiting relationships has continued to climb, reaching about eighteen million in 2018, up 29 percent since 2007. The family, the foundation of our society, is floundering and fracturing. Now guess where it is taking a toll? On our kids. As a result of families being broken, kids are stressed and depressed, living insecure lives filled with anxiety, drugs, illicit relationships, addiction to electronics, and in some cases, they reach the point of taking their own lives.

Projecting an Image

As we move into building our careers and occupying leadership positions, hours are being consumed in the pursuit of image building, on having a lifestyle of fun and consumption. We work hard to make ourselves appear to have it altogether and lose focus on character formation that comes from doing the hard and the right things. We end up not being committed to relationships or convictions and deeply held beliefs. Even worse, we ignore them. Many people do not give a serious thought to their values and beliefs or why they even matter. They think, *Who cares what I believe and value, or for that matter, what others believe and value?* Our life, however, runs on the rails of what we believe, whether we acknowledge it or not.

We live in a time when morality is free-falling. Our culture celebrates self-indulgence instead of sacrifice and self-denial. We are becoming a society addicted to everything that will give us a dopamine or an adrenaline rush. We get our high from drugs, alcohol, gaming, electronics, sexual stimulation, sports, and even the overindulgence of food!

To Live a Moral Life

Living a moral, industrious life sounds like hard work, and to many, it sounds boring. Working hard, taking personal responsibility, and thinking critically for ourselves can be difficult, and besides, we might not like what we think. Frankly, you don't have to have all the answers, but you need to have the courage to ask the crucial questions. We are masters of self-deception, and we avoid

> *Living a moral, industrious life sounds like hard work, and to many, it sounds boring.*

looking beyond the moment and the immediate future. With little regard for thought, we succumb to behavior that is governed by our emotions. What we don't realize is that culture shapes the way we feel and think. We conform to whatever is the current trend or hot topic. Lives are wasted, and our limited time on earth is spent serving the priorities of self-gratification or cultural norms.

When we fail to anchor what we do into what we believe, we get so caught up in activities that bring immediate gratification. In turn, we miss or ignore opportunities to learn and translate our beliefs into producing lasting good works that are purposeful, productive, and fulfilling.

So how do we break away from our frenetic pace of life and slow down? How do we shut off the political correctness of our culture that tries to impose the most current opinion on what is right and what is wrong, what we should think or not think, what we should do or not do?

First, we have to ask ourselves serious questions: What is important to me? What do I believe and why do I believe it? What do I need to change about the way I think? What are my values and convictions? What are the principles that guide my life? These are questions that should be constantly revisited in all seasons of life.

We also have to consider who greatly influences our lives. Who do you listen to and where do you look for truth? What are you reading? What does the media tell you, and can you trust what they say? Leadership starts when we muster enough courage to look inward and answer these questions about what defines us. We have to be sensitive to what our conscience, gifted to us by our Creator, tells us about how to distinguish right from wrong, good from evil.

By nature, we are born with the desire to be accepted by others and to fit in. Unfortunately, many of us fall into the illusion that our value is determined by others. We are more concerned about how we look on the outside—how we are being perceived by others—than how we are being shaped inside.

The Downside of Chasing after Success

As we pursue a grand lifestyle, far too many of us put in long hours, fueled by the urgent need to keep up with the Joneses. This raises our stress levels as we fight against anxiety and our fear of failure. What ultimately happens to us? We get depressed or have anxiety attacks. Many end up emotional wrecks, and life spirals downward. It is always easier to feel down than lift ourselves up. To resolve our inner morass of conflict, we can withdraw or, conversely, try to offset the long hours at work by playing hard and looking for satisfaction in entertainment and anything that gives us pleasure and excitement. Meanwhile, our health—spiritual, physical, mental, and emotional— deteriorates. Our relationships are strained.

Then there are those who are struggling in our culture and not faring well. Feeling like failures, they just cannot live up to expectations of the "haves" who seem to have it altogether by displaying an indulgent lifestyle. Unfortunately, for those in the struggling category, they are susceptible to develop a victim mentality and succumb to helplessness, insecurity, and depression, or worse. A growing segment of our population turns to drugs to numb the mind, or pornography for a temporary emotional fix, or join some cult and give their soul over to darkness.

It is easy to say to someone, "You just have to choose to slow down." But then we have to make a living. We have families that need nurture and support, bills to pay, errands to run, housekeeping chores to do, and social activities to attend. At the end of a long day, we fall into bed dead tired, feeling that there aren't enough hours in the day. We fail to invest time on things that really matter, while we yearn for some time and space to invest our energy into the important but not urgent priorities in our life. Isn't it ironic that we have so many time-saving devices compared to previous generations, yet this still happens?

Do you ever wonder what's going on? How do we get a break from all these? What needs to change? It's about time we realize that we can find the answers to these questions staring right at us in the mirror.

We need to change.

CHAPTER 6

NEVER TOO LATE TO CHANGE

Liz had every reason to fail. She grew up in the Bronx with parents who were addicted to hard drugs. As a young girl, she watched her parents self-destruct: her mother died of AIDS, while her father continued living a life of drug dependency. After the death of her mother, Liz, in her early teens then, had to fend for herself and made the street her home. She was drawn to others like her who lived only for the moment. They cared so little about tomorrow. She knew that if she continued living this way, she might repeat her mother's life and end up like her.

Things started to change when she was invited to spend the night at her friend's home. After everyone was asleep, Liz got up and wrote about her dream of having her own apartment. She wanted to have simple things that many people take for granted—privacy, heat, food, bed, and clean clothes (especially socks). She thought it must be wonderful to be able to sleep soundly, with nobody waking her up, and to be able to enjoy warm baths. *What would it take for me to fulfill my dream?* she wondered. *School. I need to go back to school.*

But which school will admit her as a freshman? Liz was turning seventeen. She was afraid that she might be too old to be a high school freshman. What were the chances that a seventeen-year-old would be able to finish four years of high school? Statistics would say she would have little to no chance.

Her dream of a better life didn't go away. One day, while sitting on a curb in New York, she was contemplating what she would do with the last of her money. *Buy a slice of pizza or take the subway back home?* Maybe she could try her luck one more time. After some searching, she finally found a school that would accept her. Determined to succeed, she finished four years of high school in two years as a straight-A student. This happened while she was living on the streets of New York City. It wasn't always easy though. She admits that there were times when she was ready to give up. What kept her going was the fear of disappointing the teachers who had invested extra effort and time to help her. These people loved her.

After completing high school, she thought about going to college. Some small scholarships were available, but she needed a big scholarship that would pay for everything. She entered a contest sponsored by the *New York Times* and wrote an essay about her life. She won! Liz received a scholarship that landed her at Harvard University. In spite of her difficult circumstances, she graduated and went on to having a clear purpose and a vision for what she wants to accomplish with her life. In her pursuit to inspire others, especially inner-city kids, she continues to tell them that their past doesn't dictate their future and that they can do a lot more about their circumstances than they might think. She now gives inspirational talks and gets invited by Fortune 500 companies as a motivational speaker. What a story of having a dream, overcoming seemingly insurmountable challenges, and working hard! Hers is also a story of forgiveness, sacrifice, and the power of love. If you want to know more about Liz Murray's story, check out her book, *Breaking Night: A Memoir of Forgiveness, Survival, and My Journey from Homeless to Harvard.*

The Power of Making the Right Choices

You can't do anything about your past, but you can help shape your future. Liz had all the cards stacked against her, but she had a dream and a hope and put her plan into action. It was hard following through. One of the things she said that struck her was about the weight of her books. She didn't think about how heavy textbooks can be. Having no permanent address, she had to carry her textbooks around with her everywhere, along with her personal belongings. But in the end, through the challenges and hardships, Liz found her life's purpose. What about us? What is stopping us from changing the course of our lives, like Liz?

What is stopping us from changing the course of our lives?

Our ability to make changes in our lives may not be as dramatic as in her case, but in the end, we are personally responsible for our decisions and actions. It is our choices and our efforts to learn, to grow, and move to action that shape our life story.

Struggling with Poverty

Many people are struggling with debt, and today there is much political talk about income disparity. Yes, some have more money than others, but the fact is very few people living in this country know what real poverty looks like. I am not dismissing those who are currently having a hard time paying the bills, but if you visit some third world countries, you will get a true picture of poverty and the hopelessness in countries that are governed by corrupt leaders. Unfortunately, we are being convinced that many of us in the Western world are victimized by the rich and are entitled to our share of the wealth we didn't earn. The younger generation is not being prepared for making a life and a living. At the same time, some from the older generation are paying the price for not sacrificing and not delaying gratification, so now they are living on the verge of poverty. The government can't be the savior of people who do not take personal responsibility and put any effort to work. Of course, we need to have compassion for the people who are struggling, and we should be generous. But depending on the government for one's survival is not the answer.

Is Money Evil?

The story of the rich young ruler as told in the Gospel of Matthew 19 can be contrasted with that of the poor widow who gave all she had in Luke 21. This presents the picture that income disparity is not a new issue. It's been happening for thousands of years. What we do with wealth is a moral and spiritual issue. There is nothing wrong with money, but you cannot count on it to make you happy. It is the *love of money* but not the money itself that is the root of all evil (see 1 Timothy 6:10). What the Bible speaks against is greed. The fact is many wealthy people live miserable lives. Jesus said, "Truly, I say to you, only with difficulty will a rich person enter the kingdom of heaven" (Matthew 19:23).

Time for a New Mindset

To break free from the forces of our past failures and to resist the pull of our culture, we need to adopt a new mindset and worldview. The power to achieve personal transformation and lasting character change comes from our Creator. As creatures created in God's image, we are created with the incredible potential to change. Many, like Liz Murray, have come from very difficult circumstances and have made substantial contributions to the society. Joni Eareckson-Tada particularly comes to mind. At age seventeen, she dove into the water and broke her neck. Her spinal cord was severed because of the accident, and she became a paraplegic. Recently I finished reading *Heaven: Your Real Home*, one of her forty books, and came away inspired by her deep, abiding faith as she shared about her struggles with pain and physical limitations. Not being able to move her body from the neck down didn't stop her from becoming a great artist who paints using a brush and her teeth. She once signed a book for us with a pen in her teeth, and her writing is much better than mine. Joni is an accomplished artist, author, singer, radio personality, and founder of Joni and Friends ministry. Her organization provides wheelchairs for the disabled all over the world. Read her book. You will be blessed and inspired and will get a glimpse of God's amazing work in her life.

Every person has amazing potential to achieve and succeed. But does success always equal fulfillment? We were not made for a short-term life but for one that stretches into eternity. In Matthew 16:26, we read, "For what will it profit a man if he gains the whole world and forfeits his soul? Or what shall a man give in return for his soul?" The leader must think that her impact and influence should reach far beyond her private life. This is true in my case because there are many people in my life who have already passed into eternity yet continue to influence and impact my life.

Facing Our Problem

How do we achieve a fulfilled life? It comes from humbly acknowledging that we have a problem. We are all born broken and will stay broken until we do something about it. There is a pervasive focus on sensual gratification and self-centeredness, alluring to all of us. But can we really be in control? Think of all the things that happen in our world that we have no control over. We should be actively pursuing God's saving grace and purpose for our lives so that we can be positioned for radical change. Our past can be used to shape our future. As I pointed out in the story of Joshua, God will and does use our past, even the most difficult circumstances, to shape our character and our future. So when we genuinely recognize that God is God and we're not, and that we are lost and in need of a Savior, namely God's Son, Jesus Christ, then we are positioned by God's grace to make real, lasting changes in our lives. Why? Because we make changes when we are convicted that our lives are broken and that we need a new and clean heart. King David, after his adulterous affair with Bathsheba, had a change of heart and prayed, "Create a clean heart in me O God, and renew a right spirit within me" (Psalm 51:10). God extends forgiveness and grace when we face and repent of the flaws and brokenness in our character. We still need to take personal responsibility for faults and failures. Leadership starts within us, and the fulfilled leader is one who serves the Master by serving others. Self-awareness and knowledge should come first! We can't change until we see that we need to.

Like Inspecting a House

Have you ever bought a house? Let me tell you how my wife and I go through the house-hunting process. We start by looking in a specific area and hiring a Realtor. Our next step is to check out the house. Lucky for me, my wife takes great notes on everything so we don't overlook anything or forget what we saw during our viewing. We see what we like and note the things that need to be fixed or changed and try to determine whether it is worth the time, effort, and money to proceed and make an offer. After this step, we hire an inspector to look at things below the surface to assure the house is structurally sound. In a sense, we are paying the inspector to give us bad news, if any. Why? Because we need to know the truth, good and bad, what is seen and unseen. Even after buying a house, we subject it to periodic inspections to make sure that our home is in good working order. If and when we discover something that needs attention, we fix it before the problem gets bigger. We can ignore, for example, a small leak in our house, but if we continually ignore it or put off fixing it for too long, it will become a bigger problem that will cost us more money to fix.

If we can do this for our house, why not our own lives? We should look carefully into our lives to see if there are some things that need to change. Our lives need to go through periodic inspection—introspection—too. We need to have the courage and humility to see ourselves as we truly are. It is wise to clean up our own act before we start fixing somebody else. When we have problems with others, we often exclude ourselves from any personal responsibility and accountability. It is always their fault. Yes, it's far easier to blame others. But this needs to change. We should not be afraid to ask ourselves, *What responsibility do I have for this problem? Did I contribute to this issue?* A good leader is one who can see his or her own faults and shortcomings.

What does introspection entail? It means examining our choices, setting priorities, and discovering our unique calling. We cannot complete this process overnight though. Sometimes we need the help of another—a pastor, a good friend, a coach, or perhaps a counselor. A professional can help you draw things out in the open and help you discover an effective approach to change. In the end, however, you make the choices and decide if you will change and redirect your course.

Small Steps, Big Changes

You can make big changes by taking small, incremental steps. Given the choice, we all want a quick fix to our problems. Is it any wonder that we see fitness magazines in checkout counter entice readers with, "Lose 20 pounds in 30 days"? This has invaded our TV too! "Buy this machine and get your dream body!" What the advertisements fail to mention is the importance of hard work, discipline, and mental toughness to make permanent lifestyle changes. Our life improves only when we commit to make daily changes. That's the way we build habits that in many ways define our life. Someone has said, "You will not change your life unless or until you are committed to doing something every day."

A couple years ago, I decided I would try this theory out. In my goal to build more strength, I started by doing something simple: ten push-ups every morning. I did that for a couple weeks, then moved that number up and started doing other exercises and stretches. I also walk my dog a couple miles every day. Today, two years later, my morning routine now includes doing one hundred push-ups, along with other strength-building routines and stretching. As an interesting side benefit, I lost some weight and now weigh a little less than I did in high school! Another habit I acquired years ago was reading through the entire Bible every year. Part of my morning routine includes Bible reading and prayer, and I have read the Bible through multiple times by reading a few chapters every day.

How about you? What can you do to make something like this happen? It may be as simple as having a set time for getting up and going to bed. It may be giving up a particular type of food that you know is not good for you. It may be making sure that you are getting enough rest every day. We should not minimize the benefits of rest, because it impacts our health in many ways. Studies show that seven to eight hours sleep is optimal for most people. (However, while it might be obvious that too little sleep impacts us negatively, too much sleep also has a negative effect.) The main point here is that the daily practice of good habits will change us over time. Time is the key. Will we choose to invest our time wisely or waste it? The apostle Paul gave good advice about transformation in Romans 12:1–2:

> I appeal to you brothers, by the mercies of God, to present your bodies as a living sacrifice, holy and acceptable to God, which is your spiritual worship. Do not be conformed to this world, but be transformed by the renewal of your mind, that by testing you may discern what is the will of God, what is good acceptable and perfect.

The Past Does Not Dictate the Future

Many struggle with the problems of the past, dealing with guilt, bad memories, rejection, and, ironically, even success. Some feel victimized by circumstances that they cannot alter and feel paralyzed or inadequate, feeling hopeless to create a better future. Granted, our past and our circumstances do play a role in how we have been shaped as individuals. In some instances, it can be a painful experience to remember a failure, but then we should deal with it. As J. M. Barrie, the author of *Peter Pan*, puts it, "The life of every man is a diary in which he means to write one story, and writes another: and his humblest hour is when he compares the volume as it is with what he vowed to make it." It seems like nothing could be worse than looking back on life with remorse and regret. But perhaps, with help, we can have hope in the future and choose to make changes in how we think and what we do. A portion of this life is suffering and disappointment, but unless there are deep wounds that require professional help, we can choose to stop being victims of our past. Most often, we already know what we should do or stop doing but often avoid making the hard decisions and choosing to do what's moral. Moral choice asks, "How do we invest our God-given talent, time, and resources?" Moral choice undergirds our whole life. Will we choose to focus only on ourselves and what we want, or are we willing to look beyond ourselves? A leader's purpose is to bring out the best in themselves and in others.

Don't Be Fooled by Success

We look around and see people who seem to have their lives all together. They have great jobs, good kids, a nice house, and what appears to be a fulfilling life. But is it as it seems? We can have all the money in the world and still have our lives fall apart. Some people chase pleasure, entertainment, and a lifestyle that is all about them. There are those who seek power and promote self-aggrandizement. But rich or poor, we came into the world with nothing, and that's also the way we will depart. No matter how much money someone has, he or she is not immune to despair. We're not shocked when we hear of someone homeless dying on the street but are shocked when seemingly successful people tragically take their own lives.

We cannot find the answer to living a fulfilled life by relying on our own wisdom and willpower. It all boils down to the God question: is God God, or are we god? The answer is found in seeking meaning and purpose. On our own, we might find something to devote our lives to, but is it lasting or is it temporary? Is there a life after this?

This is where faith and knowledge enter in. We live in a world of anxiety and stress where many are suffering from depression and hopelessness. Know that, as a leader, when we pursue purpose and meaning in our lives and then bring faith into the equation, we will be swimming against the current of our culture. We will be subject to pushback, scorn, and ridicule. The working out of our leadership and character will continue to be shaped by suffering through trials and difficult times. Like Joshua, our faith and trust and our reliance on God should guide our thinking and behavior in day-to-day leadership. Our personal growth and spiritual growth are developed as we learn to navigate through challenging times and from the effort we

> *We can have all the money in the world and still have our lives fall apart.*

make consciously. We can learn from reading, listening to trusted sources, and putting into practice behaviors that eventually become ingrained as good habits.

We all have turning points in our lives when choices are made that have long-lasting if not lifelong consequences. Os Guinness, in his book *The Call*, gives us some insight into some of the turning points in life:

> Teenagers feel it as the world of freedom beyond home and secondary school beckons with a dizzying range of choices.
>
> Graduate students confront it when the excitement of "the world is my oyster" is chilled by the thought that opening up one choice means closing down others.
>
> Those in their thirties know it when daily work assumes its own brute reality beyond their earlier considerations of the wishes of their parents, the

fashions of their peers, and the allure of salary and career prospects.

People in midlife face it when a mismatch between their gifts and their work reminds them daily that they are square pegs in round holes. Can they see themselves doing that for the rest of their lives?

Mothers feel it when their children grow up and they wonder which high purpose will fill the void in the next stage of their lives.

People in their forties and fifties with enormous success suddenly come up against it when their accomplishments raise questions concerning the social responsibility of their success and, deeper still, the purpose of their lives.

Those in later years often face it again. What does life add up to? Were their successes real and were they worth the trade-offs?

Change for the Better

So how do we create change? We decide what needs to change and then change. Easier said than done, right? Much of what we talked about in the previous chapter regarding the state of our culture can be linked back to the four traits needed to be a good leader: character, competence, conviction, and courage. There are many things about us that we cannot change—our race, where we were born, our parents, our personality, our physical traits, talents, and the things that come naturally to us. Most of us didn't have a say about what school we attended and the traditions and values we were exposed to growing up. Things that happened in our past—whether good or bad—helped shaped who we are today.

The good news is it's not a dead end. We can reshape our character, broaden our competencies, deepen our convictions, and grow our courage. When we do this, we can change something bigger: our future.

CHAPTER 7

CHARACTER

Leaders come in all shapes and sizes—as introverts or extroverts, with different backgrounds and experiences, and with unique combinations of talents and strengths. However, regardless of position or status in life, four things contribute to what truly makes a leader: character, competence, conviction, and courage.

Let's start with character. Its genesis is the leader's heart. Remember what I said earlier—that leadership is an inside-out job? Leadership begins at the core of our being. Our core is influenced by what we allow from the outside to affect us on the inside. We are all shaped by our outside environment and the experiences we've had in all the seasons of life. Much of how we think, feel, and respond is influenced by external factors. On the other hand, have you ever thought about how we decide and make choices about right and wrong? Can we regulate what we think about? The answer to this question is yes ... and no. Random thoughts come into our minds many times, but we can become conscious of good and bad thoughts. With on-purpose thinking, we can isolate our thoughts. We can discern and make choices about what is right and what is wrong and what is good and what is evil. We have the ability to examine them and have the capacity to acknowledge what is wrong and redirect our thoughts.

Where's the Control Center?

So where does our ability to choose what to think about come from? It begins at the control center—the heart. I don't mean the physical organ that pumps blood through the network of arteries and veins in our body. It is also not the heart we think about during Valentine's Day. I'm talking about the control center, the heart or spirit that distinguishes us from animals. The heart or our spirit (I will use these terms interchangeably) is where our will or our personal autonomy can control the thought life. We cannot completely control thoughts that pop into our minds, but we can decide if we want to ponder and meditate on a thought. We have the power to redirect our thinking. Thoughts can be for good or for evil, and how we respond to them determines our direction and behavior over the long haul. And the condition of the our heart is what ultimately defines our character.

The prophet Jeremiah said, "The heart is deceitful above all things and desperately sick, who can understand it?" (see Jeremiah 17:9). This verse implies that it is in the heart where decisions are first made. No wonder Jesus said, "What comes out of a person defiles him. For from within, out of the heart comes evil thoughts, sexual immorality, theft, murder, adultery, coveting, wickedness, deceit, sensuality, envy, slander, pride, foolishness. All these things come from within and they defile a person" (Mark 7:20–23). *But I don't do any of these things*, you protest. But if you look carefully at each of these, you will realize that you might be more guilty than you think. Yes, some sins seem worse than others, and perhaps they are, but we must be aware that we are so susceptible to deceiving ourselves. One deception leads to another. One lie leads to another, and before we know it, lies accumulate to build an entire belief system that is false. Deception builds as we linger on thoughts that appeal to our baser instincts, which is when we start to rationalize and justify our thoughts. Then our false thinking leads to a belief that ultimately translates to action. In the book *Leadership and Self-Deception,* produced by the Arbinger Institute, we read:

Self-deception is like this: It blinds us to the true causes of problems and once we're blind all the "solutions" we can think of will actually make matters worse. Whether at work or at home, self-deception obscures the truth about ourselves, corrupts our view of others and our circumstances and inhibits our ability to make wise and helpful decisions. To the extent that we are self-deceived, both our happiness and our leadership are undermined.

The Mind and the Heart

There is no question that the mind and the heart work together to forge our character. The mind stores memories of the past, operates in the present (even when we are not consciously aware), and can envision a future. When we make choices and decisions where we intuitively know right from wrong, it leads back to the spirit of our being. Much of what we know about right and wrong, we are taught or we learn from experience. Nevertheless, the choice to say yes or no is dictated by the heart, where free will resides. Our mind and heart send messages to each other, back and forth. How does this happen? We are bombarded daily by sound bites, video clips, and words in print or on screen. As our mind is being fed information, our heart processes it. This gives us all the more reason to guard what we allow ourselves to listen to and watch. The Bible warns us, "Guard your heart above all else for it determines the course of your life" (Proverbs 4:23 NLT).

When I was a young man, I learned a simple definition of God: "God was a Spirit with all the highest perfections." God is a Spirit, and we were born in His image. So we, having been created in the image of God, are spiritual beings, but unlike God, we are far from being perfect! Our imperfections are the result of Adam and Eve's sin. We received a flawed heart (spirit) as our inheritance, a heart governed by the self that left to its own devices will result in destruction. The fact is people are born defective—totally dependent on others, helpless, and self-centered. When babies need attention, they take no thought of whether the people around them may be inconvenienced. They will cry until they get what they want. From the moment we come into the world, we are self-centered, and if left without any guidance growing up, we will live the rest of our lives concerned only with ourselves. Young children, left without correction and direction, will turn into adults who will refuse to take personal responsibility for their character and behavior.

> *The fact is people are born defective—totally dependent on others, helpless, and self-centered.*

In Search of the Truth

The antidote to self-deception, or any deception, is truth. First, there is truth we can easily verify. For instance, the law of gravity is true. We can choose to say that gravity is not real and willingly step off the roof of a skyscraper, but we would soon find out that our mistaken belief about gravity would not change the truth about the law of gravity. Second, there is truth that we can prove instantly. We could say we have a quarter in our pocket and reach in our pocket and produce a quarter to prove the truth of having a quarter. Third, there is moral truth that is immediately evident and other times needs to be verified from a reliable source of truth. Sadly, some people believe that truth is relative. They say that truth cannot be defined or, at best, truth can only be arrived at by consensus. That is, we all ultimately choose what we want to believe, and that makes it the truth. Frankly, without a grounding in truth, life is irrelevant. The fact is we all believe something whether we can articulate it or not.

Jordan Peterson, in his book *12 Rules for Life*, said this: "All people serve their ambitions. In that matter there are no atheists. There are only people who know and don't know what God (god) they serve." Peterson continues by saying, "For the big lie, you first need the little lie." We start with "little white lies," or at least that's what we call them. They're harmless, we may say, but deep down inside us, we know that we are wrong. We convince ourselves of this fact until we ultimately act on them. Then we have to lie or deceive ourselves to justify our actions. Lies build on themselves. When we get into the habit of lying, our conscience becomes numb to the truth. We believe the lie

> *When we get into the habit of lying, our conscience becomes numb to the truth.*

because, in our pride and selfishness, we want to serve the self. We become our own little god, believing only what we want to be right.

Truth Is Truth

Moral truth is not about how we feel or what we think or believe is truth. Actually, truth is totally indifferent to what we think. In other words, truth is truth whether we believe it or not. What we as flawed humans do is try to reshape reality to fit our desires and establish a truth to fit what we want to believe. Dallas Willard, a renowned philosopher at USC, writes, "Even when a child feels a tug on his conscience that he has done something wrong and feels guilty and whether he or she knows it or not, they have acknowledged that there is moral truth in the universe." In other words, if anyone knows that she ought to do something, but does the opposite, she is validating that moral truth exists.

While I will talk more fully about convictions in another chapter, let me mention two convictions that I hold on to: 1) absolute moral truth exists; and 2) the Bible is absolutely true. The psalmist in Psalm 119:160 said, "The sum of your Word is truth, and every one of your righteous rules endures forever." For me, my source of moral truth comes from what I believe and trust is truth from the pages of the Bible. Truth and trust go hand in hand. The effective leader needs both. We should have a reliable source of moral truth and not depend on opinion that so readily pervades the ideology that is spewed forth today. If there is no source for moral truth, then we revert to opinion, and then anything we want to believe is truth. We know that opinions change more frequently than the weather, and believing opinions can lead to chaos. We see it all the time in the culture, the workplace, education, politics of today, and, sadly, sometimes in our churches.

The way of truth is not easy. First, many do not want to hear truth, especially if it requires change and if it means denying ourselves and having to submit to a higher authority. Second, when confronted face-to-face with truth, it can be convicting and painful. The writer of Hebrews in the New Testament writes in Hebrews 4:12:

> For the word of God is living and active, sharper than any two edged-sword piercing to the division of soul and of spirit, of joints and marrow and discerning the thoughts and intentions of the heart.

When we see ourselves as we really are, that we are indeed morally lost, and become remorseful and aware of our need for cleansing, only then will we be in the position to be forgiven. By seeking truth and with the blinders of self-deception and pride removed, we can be open to truth. When we willingly place our trust and faith in Jesus Christ, recognizing He is Lord, we can commit to learning truth and following through by being obedient to truth. Only then will our heart and character as a leader be transformed.

There are many verses about truth in the Bible. Jesus said, "I am the way the truth and the life" (John 14:6). The servant leader's edge is in diligently seeking the virtue of moral excellence that springs from the inner core, when he or she surrenders his or her heart to the *true truth*. When we commit to truth, we must walk our talk. We must realize that we are not the center of the universe. God is. His incarnate Son came to earth so that our faulty hearts and our deadened spirits could be brought to life. We are more than physical beings taking up space on earth; we are spiritual beings made in the image of God so that our spirit can be united with His to bring us life and truth.

It was not so long ago when the majority in this country had at least a basic understanding of God and the Bible and respected the Christian faith. In 1960, a Chicago Public High School, William Howard Taft, published a code written by the student council that honored God and promoted good character. Two of the six principles state the following:

> *Respect for God.* This principle reminds us that the true aim of one's life is not wealth, fame, comfort, honor, or even success. It is God. History and literature all indicate that humans live for a variety of reasons, yet no aim is more exalted or sound than living for God in whom rests humankind's ultimate happiness. The history and various practices of our government attest to the fact that our democracy is founded on faith in God. Our cherished rights are inalienable because they come from God. Communism is vicious precisely because it denies God. By denying God, communism is able to usurp all rights to itself, leaving the individual without rights and therefore without dignity—a slave of the state. For many reasons then, the thinking student will always be mindful of the motto, "In God we trust."
>
> *Character development.* Today, there is too much stress on the development of personality. There can be no true personality where there is not first a substantial character. Personality is but the external reflection of a person's inner character. The need today is for the development of character. The student who is sincere, responsible, considerate of his fellows, willing to give of his time and efforts, who has a fine sense of values—in a word, the student who has a genuine character—is bound to have at the same time an attractive personality.

Can you imagine a document like this written for today's public schools? Not a chance! Yet not that many years ago, most people in North America and Western Europe had an understanding of

Judeo-Christian values that shaped our culture. Today, much of those values have deteriorated and diminished. If you have the courage to believe and live out these principles, you may well be accused of bigotry and discrimination by others. When a person, however, with a godly character and conviction steps out courageously, he can make a huge difference and impact by the way he leads.

William Wilberforce

William Wilberforce allowed his faith to shape the culture. His grand purpose consisted of two initiatives: 1) end slave trade; and 2) introduce the reformation of manners. But he faced a daunting task. There was much economic benefit brought about by slave trade, not only to England but to other European countries, as well as the United States.

Who was this man? William Wilberforce was born in 1759 and was only twenty years old when he became a member of the Parliament. Slightly built, about five foot three, and in poor health, he wasn't an imposing figure, but he later became a force to be reckoned with.

Wilberforce admitted he did little in the Parliament in his first years. In his words, he said, "I did nothing ... nothing to any purpose. My own distinction, was my darling project." That whole attitude changed when he began to reflect deeply on his life. The end result was he experienced a spiritual rebirth. He engaged in a rigorous self-examination that led him to think in terms of what it was to be a serious Christian. He was concerned about the use of his time. He did not want to get caught up and engage in endless dinner parties that were full of vain and useless conversations. He began to see his life's purpose summed up in his two grand initiatives—to end slave trade and restore manners.

J. Douglas Holladay, writing about Wilberforce, listed seven characteristics or principles that defined Wilberforce's life.[1]

---

[1] This narrative can be found in Character Counts, a book edited by Os Guinness and published by Baker Publishing Group in 1999.

First, Wilberforce's whole life was animated by a deeply held, personal faith in Jesus Christ. Wilberforce and his colleagues were motivated by a robust personal faith in a living God who is concerned with individual human lives, justice, and transformation of human societies. He had a powerful sense of the power and presence of God, giving them vision, courage, and perspective to choose their issues and stand against powerful interests aligned against them. Wilberforce, along with his friends, viewed himself as a pilgrim on a mission of mercy, never defining his identity or purposes by the flawed values of his age. This transcendent perspective made him the freest of men and therefore the most threatening force against the status quo.

Second, Wilberforce had a deep sense of calling that grew into the conviction that he was to exercise his spiritual purpose in the realm of his secular responsibility. Too often, people of faith draw a dichotomy between the spiritual and the secular. Religious or spiritual activities are considered a lofty calling, while secular involvements are viewed with disdain and are believed to have little to do with true spirituality. Those with true spiritual sensitivities are urged to pursue "religious" affairs, such as ministry, rather than face the tough, complex struggles inherent in the swirl of business or politics.

Third, Wilberforce was committed to the strategic importance, to a band of like-minded friends devoted to working together in chosen ventures. History bears witness to the influence of individuals combining energies and skill to achieve a shared objective. His particular band of associates was tagged "The Saints" by their contemporaries in Parliament—uttered by some with contempt, while by others with deep admiration. The achievement of Wilberforce's vision is largely attributable to the value he and his colleagues placed on harnessing their diverse skills while submitting their egos for the greater public good.

Fourth, Wilberforce believed deeply in the power of ideas and moral beliefs to change culture through a campaign of sustained public persuasion. He and his friends presented a petition to Parliament signed by 10 percent of the British people. Wilberforce persuaded the famous potter Joshua Wedgewood to create a special medallion. At the center of the plate was a kneeling slave in shackles, and inscribed around the edge was the question: "Am I not Man and a Brother?" They also published books, periodicals, and tracts to win the hearts and minds. All this was to raise awareness and provoke conversation.

Fifth, Wilberforce was willing to pay a steep cost for his courageous public stands and was remarkably persistent in pursuing his life task. For forty years, Wilberforce labored for what some thought was unachievable—the total eradication of slavery from the British empire. Suffering defeat upon defeat, he would not be denied. Only three days before his death in July 1833, Parliament made one of the greatest moral decisions by a legislative body in history, a decision counter to its own economic advantage. Wilberforce, in his commitment to enduring virtues, had prevailed, despite the cost to his health, reputation, and political ambitions.

Sixth, Wilberforce's labors and faith were grounded in a genuine humility rather than a blind fanaticism. It was characteristic of Wilberforce that he worked comfortably not only with friends but with those opposed to his views on faith and society. His character remained the same. Without being defensive or sanctimonious, he expressed his beliefs in a natural and straightforward manner. Wilberforce, while committed to deeply passionate causes, had his identity and contentment anchored elsewhere. So he was a man at peace in the storms of his times, one who integrated every facet of his life and thought in the perspective of faith.

Seventh, Wilberforce forged strategic partnerships for the common good, irrespective of differences over methods, ideology, or religious beliefs. He attacked evils vigorously but worked with respect and tolerance for people of very diverse allegiances.

Many great leadership lessons can be learned from Wilberforce's life that have application to our world today. If we are to lead and thrive in the reality of our post-Christian culture, we need to be ready to persevere, be clear about our convictions, and learn to lead with truth, courage, perseverance, competence, and humility. Jesus gives us this command, "Go … I am sending you out like lambs among wolves" (Luke 10:3). We need to lead with strength of character, to know who we are, what we want to accomplish, what we believe, and why we believe it and put it in practice so we can lead others.

Evidence of Truth

Look at the universe, the vastness of space, the earth and its vegetation and living creatures and its vast geographic landscape. It is too much of a stretch (at least for me) to think it all happened randomly. Think of the span of our solar system as measured in terms of the speed of light—seven hundred light minutes. This translates to about eight billion miles. Our galaxy is one hundred thousand light-years in breadth, and there are many galaxies in the universe. It's mind-boggling! Some people believe it's incorrect to say, "In the beginning, God created the heavens and the earth." Yet He did. Much more has been written that supports my point from those much better educated and informed than I in the field of science that could offer much more. We struggle to comprehend what science says about space and the universe, but how can we believe all this just happened by some random chance? Why is it so difficult to believe that there is an Intelligent Being when we try to take in the magnitude of our universe? The psalmist says, "The heavens declare the glory of God, and the sky above proclaims his handiwork" (Psalm 19:1).

Recognizing Who We Are

The Creator has made us and gifted us with natural talents. This is true whether we believe in God or not. In many cases, we have not given conscious thought as to what our talents might be. How can we put talents to work if we don't know what they actually are? What we should realize is that we put natural talents to work every day. Sometimes we recognize it in others when we see a person do something with relative ease while it may seem difficult for us. To that person, we may say she is just a natural. To me, a sure sign of the sanctity of our lives is revealed by our talents.

The Gallup Corporation has developed a tool to help identify talent themes unique to an individual. The tool to identify talent themes is explained in the book *The StrengthFinder 2.0* (recently renamed to *CliftonStrengths34*). In the back of the book is an access code that will allow you to go online and take an assessment based on individual input. The outcome of the assessment identifies thirty-four talent themes in rank order. The top five themes are identified as signature themes, and out of this grouping, only one in thirty-three million people have the same order of talents just in their top five. Add the next twenty-nine themes and then pour into the mix our personality, our cognitive ability (IQ), our relationships, and other personal and unique experiences. You won't find anyone in the seven billion plus people on planet Earth exactly like you.

A good place to start assessing ourselves is to answer the questions, *Who am I? How am I wired? Why am I here? What do I want?* The more I read about how our brains and bodies function, it strengthens my belief in a Creator who made us. How do we best get in touch with who we are? One, by engaging our heart and using our brain and some of the tools available to help us identify what makes us tick. As for finding purpose and meaning, we should go to the Creator who made us in the first place. It might sound trite and simplistic, but it is not. It requires soul searching, introspection, careful thinking, exercising faith, and believing that the Spirit of God will work in conjunction with our spirit to guide us to truth and light. The wise man said, "The spirit of man is the lamp of the LORD, searching all his innermost parts" (Proverbs 20:27).

Time: To Invest or to Spend?

The process of developing a leader's heart and character is ongoing, and we must engage our hearts and minds on a day-to-day basis. Time is a gift that we all have in equal proportions. Whether a person has billions in the bank or just a penny in his pocket, we all get allotted twenty-four hours a day. In the early part of the nineteenth century, British author Arnold Bennett wrote *How to Live on Twenty-Four Hours a Day*. Here's what he had to say nearly two hundred years ago:

> The proverb, that time is money, underestimates the case. Time is the inexplicable raw material of everything. Without it, nothing is possible. The supply of time is truly a daily miracle. You wake up in the morning, and lo! Your purse is magically filled with 24 hours of the unmanufactured tissue of your life. It is yours. Which of us has not been saying to himself; *I shall alter this or that, when I have a little more time?* Which of us is not haunted by the feeling that as the years slip by, and we have not yet been able to get our lives in proper working order. We have and we always have had, all the time there is.

The point is that struggling with how to use our time is not new. In spite of all the time-saving devices we have today, there is just not enough time in the day. In our twenty-first-century world, I wonder sometimes if some of these time-saving conveniences really save any time. Take email for example. It's amazing that we can be almost anywhere in the world and connect with others, and they in turn can respond almost instantly. If we go back to Arnold Bennett's day, mail used to take days to reach its intended recipient, yet the people then survived nonetheless. I'm not suggesting we go back to the nineteenth century. On the other hand, how many emails do we have to sort through and trash

Are we spending [time] on things that don't really matter, or are we investing it on things that will last for eternity?

every day? But let's go back to the big picture: What are we doing with our time? Are we spending it on things that don't really matter, or are we investing it on things that will last for eternity?

The Importance of Order

In the beginning, God created order. (Actually, in the beginning, God created everything.) There remains order in God's universe today. And the sobering fact is that, in the end, none of us are getting out of this world alive. All the stuff that keeps us busy, many of the urgent things we feel compelled to do, will end up discarded like so much of yesterday. So thinking about the purpose of our lives is a crucial investment so we can avoid looking back with regret. Again, we are not here just to take up space. What we do with our gift of time must be a conscious choice. Are we here on earth just to be happy and have fun? Some may think so and end up drifting through life. Deep down, many people want to make a difference through their ability to lead, serve, influence, inspire, and impact others for a greater good. There are also some who center their lives around causes, careers, travel, adventure, or just fun. Many work day in, day out for that ultimate goal—retirement. They work only to reach this stage so they can have a carefree life to travel, engage in hobbies, and pursue leisure. Unfortunately, this kind of life doesn't always satisfy. As Solomon would say, "That all is vanity and chasing after the wind" (Ecclesiastes 1:14).

Leaving a Legacy

Many leaders fail because they exhibit a major flaw in their character. We are all vulnerable to temptation, and many a leader has been ruined by falling into some immoral temptation, and lives have been ruined. It is difficult for a leader to recover once she is found to have done something immoral. Are you afraid that you might find yourself in this position? How can we protect ourselves and those we lead? One way is to recognize the way we might be susceptible to moral failure and establish safeguards against temptations.

Billy Graham, the great evangelist, took the pitfalls of temptation seriously. He brought his leadership team together and talked about the recurring problems that plagued high-profile people in

Christian ministry, especially his counterparts. As his team studied the problems, they identified four major issues: 1) misusing God's money; 2) engaging in sexual immorality; 3) badmouthing others doing similar work; and 4) exaggerating accomplishments.

The leadership team realized that if they weren't careful, sinning in any of these four areas could destroy the whole ministry and do irreparable harm to not just Billy Graham but the whole Christian message. It was from this work at the beginnings of Billy Graham's ministry that the team came up with the Modesto Manifesto,[2] highlighting these four action points:

> We will never criticize, condemn, or speak negatively of others.
>
> We will be accountable, particularly in the handling of finances, with integrity according to the highest business standards.
>
> We will tell the truth and be thoroughly honest, especially in reporting statistics.
>
> We will be exemplary in morals ... clear, clean and careful to avoid any appearance of impropriety.

They were wise to create the Modesto Manifesto to protect their ministry and the Christian message. To my knowledge, there has never been a hint of a moral scandal connected to the Billy Graham Evangelistic Association, and his son Franklin is keeping their unblemished reputation intact.

Leaders, know your weaknesses and vulnerabilities and make decisions upfront to put safeguards in place to preserve and build character. The leader's effectiveness is grounded in character of truth and moral excellence. Character development is the ongoing work of every leader, and in the end, character is the signature of every leader's legacy.

---

[2] A more complete story of the creation of the Modesto Manifesto can be found in *The Leadership Secrets of Billy Graham* by Harold Myra and Marshall Shelley, a book published by Zondervan in 2005.

CHAPTER 8

COMPETENCE

Abraham Lincoln had humble beginnings. Born in a one-room cabin in Kentucky, his family had meager resources. They moved from Kentucky to southern Indiana, where he grew up on a family farm. They left Kentucky for Indiana because the former supported slavery while the latter did not. As was common in rural areas, especially what was then known as the frontier, Lincoln received little formal education. He worked hard on the farm, and stories were told about his skill with an ax. Abraham Lincoln was self-taught and obviously disciplined, as much of his "formal" education he learned on his own from his reading, in particular the Bible, which he often read to his siblings. He also would practice preaching by repeating sermons he had heard. He enjoyed telling stories. Early in his life, Lincoln might not have known he was already being shaped for his future in leadership.

Lincoln's Long Road to Success

Lincoln learned much from his own struggles and tragedies. He lost his mother when he was just nine years old after the family moved to Indiana. He also lost a brother who died in infancy, and later, an older sister. Troubles and hard work were just part of growing up and were instrumental in shaping his character, mind, and work ethic. Later still, the family moved once again to Illinois. When young Abe turned twenty-one, after helping his father establish a farm, he set off on his own. As Lincoln forged his own path, he worked in various jobs. He became a boatman, a store clerk, a surveyor, a soldier, and eventually a lawyer in the state of Illinois. He persevered and self-studied law, and on September 9, 1836, the Illinois Supreme Court gave Lincoln an exam and issued him a license to practice law. He was elected to the state legislature at twenty-five years old, the beginning of his political career. This ultimately led him to become the president of the United States. Lincoln's development was shaped by his environment and family, but he put much effort into developing his mind. As you may know, Lincoln was not successful in everything he did, but he persevered. He experienced major setbacks and failures before tasting success. Here's a brief summary of his highs and lows:

1831—Failed in business
1832—Ran for state legislature and lost
1832—Lost his job and wanted to get into law school but couldn't get in
1833—Borrowed money to start a business, went bankrupt, and spent the next seventeen years paying off the debt
1834—Ran for state legislature and won
1835—Was engaged to be married, but his fiancée died
1836—Suffered from a nervous breakdown and was bedridden for six months
1838—Ran for speaker of the state legislature and lost
1843—Ran for Congress and lost
1846—Ran for Congress and won
1848—Ran for re-election and lost
1849—Sought the job of land officer in his home state but was rejected
1856—Ran for US Senate and lost
1858—Ran for US Senate again and lost
1860—Elected president of the United States

Abraham Lincoln ended up being one of the greatest presidents, if not the greatest president, of the United States. He persevered and never gave up and constantly invested time to learn. He took it upon himself to sharpen his intellect and to learn from his difficult life experiences. His failures could have caused him to give up on his vocational pursuits, but he pressed on. His work ethic was strong, and his honesty, legendary. He was humble and was willing to poke fun at himself too. "Honest Abe" developed a good mind and a strong character. The lesson we can learn from his life is to never stop learning and growing—physically, intellectually, emotionally, and, most important, spiritually. Abraham Lincoln made critical and brave decisions during the Civil War and after the war by not letting emotions get out of control and laying the groundwork for the South to be reconciled with the North. He saved the union. My point of recounting Lincoln's life is not to disparage education but to underscore the fact that we have to take responsibility for our personal development, and education alone does not guarantee success.

Abraham Lincoln gained competence in leadership through the years. Anybody who wants to do the same should be prepared to devote themselves fully to grow. A leader invests in the development of the mind.

It All Starts in the Mind

Imagination and ideas are spawned in the mind. Our minds can paint a picture and imagine things. Someone has said that the mind is more of a picture gallery than a debating chamber. We can see things in our mind's eye before they become reality. That's why a leader needs to cast a vision for the future. As a visionary, she is able to see what years ahead may look like to the point where she can describe it like it already happened. Depending on a person's state of the heart and mind, she is capable of envisioning the best and the worst out of a situation. For example, the compassionate person sees a suffering and a hungry world and develops a plan for how food can be delivered to the poor and needy. Meanwhile, a dictator sees scores of people who can be killed or controlled to deliver a twisted message to his enemies. Yes, left to ourselves, we are capable of doing the worst. Only when our hearts and minds are in tune and engaged with the power of God's spirit can we see with selfless motives.

By the power of the Spirit of God, we must guard our minds, where self-talk happens. We need to train ourselves to challenge our thinking and to filter what our inner voice whispers to us. The mind also is the seat of our emotions, and our self-awareness determines how well we are in tune with our feelings and emotions. The mind is a place of competing forces. One part of the mind is that part where cognitive thinking is done; it is where our analytical, technical, and rational thinking takes place.

> *We need to train ourselves to challenge our thinking and to filter what our inner voice whispers to us.*

We make plans with our cognitive thinking and execute plans from our logical thinking. We also control our emotions with our mind, even though we tend to react impulsively before thinking rationally.

Our minds can easily be distracted. It takes determined effort in order to tune out competing random thoughts and impulses from encroaching on our ability to focus. The leader's ability to focus the mind is critical to help keep the main thing the main thing. Our mind is bombarded with external and internal distractions that make it difficult to think and concentrate for long periods. Thinking well requires practice and discipline.

Eliminate Distractions

There is much we can do to eliminate distractions. For one, set up an atmosphere conducive to reducing distractions. Find a place where you can be alone. For me, I have learned that my best and most productive time of the day is the early-morning hours when it is quiet and my mind is fresh. The more we get into the day, the more our minds are invaded with outside distractions. In the early morning, it is usually quiet, and I am not bombarded with calls. I am not near my phone to check texts or emails. My computer is set not to alert me to any incoming messages. I am free to think. My habit is to get up at the same time every day, go to my office, stretch and do some floor exercises, and then spend time reading my Bible, praying, and meditating. This habit of Bible reading and prayer is so important, for it takes my mind off me and brings truth into my heart and mind. Then I write, and I find I can concentrate and think clearly. My mother used to say the morning is the best part of the day. When I was a teenager, I didn't necessarily agree with her, but I do now. The way you set up your day shapes the rest of your day. Your routine at the beginning of the day is crucial for functioning well for the next twenty-four hours.

How Is Your EQ?

The leader is shaped by the accumulation of all her knowledge gained through experiences and life lessons, along with her intellectual pursuits and how she purposely develops her mind. It takes work to develop our minds, and we must take personal responsibility to learn and expand our base of knowledge. At the same time, it takes work to be self-aware and control our feelings and emotions. Years ago, we thought a person's success depended upon IQ, but many smart people do not reach the levels of success that their IQs might have predicted. Today. much has been learned around EQ, or emotional quotient. In fact, today, EQ may be more talked about than IQ. Daniel Goleman has written a book titled *Emotional Intelligence: Why It Can Matter More Than IQ*. Emotional Intelligence can be looked at as internal and external EQ: internal is all about self-awareness and self-management; external is all about social awareness and relationship management.

The emotional and feeling part of the mind operates more from the subconscious, where we are influenced by feelings, emotions, and intuitions. The subconscious mind is also where habits are ingrained to the point where we do things on automatic pilot or where we do things and make decisions without conscious thought. It's important to acknowledge our feelings—good or bad. Sometimes our feelings and emotions help keep us out of harm's way and send warning signals when we may be in danger. Sometimes our feelings are more subtle and signal us to be wary and discerning where we intuitively know that something is not right.

Conversely, emotions and feelings can also lead us into problems. While we all want to experience good feelings, we must be careful. As an example, we are naturally self-centered, so we want to feel good and crave the charge of excitement that lust, power, and greed, among other temptations bring on. Allowing these feelings and emotions to perpetuate, we succumb to destructive behaviors that lead to harm and regret. Our mind can process both good thinking and bad thinking, and it is the condition of our hearts and minds

> *If we let our emotions control us, we might make poor choices and decisions.*

that govern our conscience, which helps us discern when we are off track. It is our free will and our ability to choose that decides our volitional acts of thinking and doing, but in the end, we are responsible for our own actions and behavior.

Do We Know How to Think?

Today, many say our schools are failing us, and sometimes I might be inclined to say that our schools are teaching our kids *what* to think but not *how* to think. Where once our learning institutions taught Judeo-Christian values, now a majority of the schools are promoting pure secularism and anti-Judeo-Christian values. Many of our young people are encouraged to abandon "old ways" of thinking about moral truth and are paying a price to voice a different point of view. Too many of us are being led by our emotions instead of our cognitive thinking. True, we have a seemingly infinite amount of information through modern technology, but our world ranking in education is falling further and further behind.

However, in the past, many great thinkers and leaders did not have the advantage of attending high-ranking schools but developed their minds because they had a hunger to learn. Competent leaders learn from reading, finding time for solitude and reflection, and learning lessons from life experience. Again, leaders must take personal responsibility for developing their minds. I'm all for formal education, but we should also realize that not all notable leaders who shaped the course of history, in the past or present, enjoyed the benefits of the formal education we prize so much today.

Thoughts and feelings originate in our minds before we act on them. Both thoughts and feeling are united to inform us, but one cannot overpower the other. As James W. Sire writes, "Let your thoughts be felt and your feelings be thought." First, for the rational mind, critical and deep thinking is hard work. Unfortunately, we tend to resist hard work. Critical thinking is purposeful and intentional and requires focus and concentration. Second, the mind is where we store knowledge, but it is also where emotions and feelings color our thinking. Most of the time, our first tendency is to react emotionally rather than act responsibly. Much of what we see among pundits, especially political pundits, is emotional expression devoid of critical thinking. We are headed for problems if our lives are governed only by how we feel.

The Value of Emotions

Our emotions give our thoughts texture and passion, which releases chemicals in the body that enhance our energy and endurance. For instance, if you're frightened, your body dispenses adrenaline and cortisol. If you're happy and excited, you get dopamine and serotonin. Although much has been learned in neuroscience about the brain and how it functions, much is still unknown. Feelings assist our thinking and help seat our convictions and passions. When we think long enough about something, our thoughts eventually lead to action and behavior. To be an effective leader, one must be able to master himself and lead himself before he leads others. If we let our emotions control us, we might make poor choices and decisions. Sometimes if we are not clear in our thinking, for example, not knowing our priorities or not clearly identifying the issue, we are susceptible to making decisions based on how we feel. We may find ourselves vacillating and refusing to decide, or end up making decisions that appeal more to our feelings than reason. For a leader, this can be disastrous. Strong emotional feelings can influence our objective thinking, while on the other hand, objective rational thinking can bring our feelings and emotions under control. The key is to harmonize our cognitive thinking with our feelings. Much has been written about emotional intelligence. Understanding it is crucial for the successful leader. While I emphasize the need for deeper thinking and more critical thinking, we can't lead well without our emotions in play. The leader cannot allow her thinking to be hijacked by feelings, but the leader also cannot be dispassionate to the point of only technical, factual data leaving no room for empathy.

Emotions bring energy and life to our thinking and many times activate our passion for achievement. Emotions can bring on excitement and energy that facilitate achievement or, conversely, can trigger unbridled anger along with other more destructive emotions. Thinking and emotions should always be connected. Thinking brings on feelings, and feelings can trigger thinking. There is not one without the other.

Finally, because of the gift of thought and our ability to reason, our minds can range beyond ourselves. Many times, we are guided by our instincts but not limited by instincts or even what we take in by our five senses. Our mind can be driven by curiosity and imagination to explore the wonders of our seen and unseen world. While our mind is taking in information all the time, we can intuitively know without being consciously aware. While we are at it, just to clarify, some may confuse the mind with the brain and say that the two are the same. For our purposes, we are looking at the brain as the hardware that houses the mind, which is the software where thinking and feeling take place.

Practice Makes Perfect?

As a leader, you need to get things done. How you get things done has to do with competence. Competence is acquired by investing in learning and practice. Practice develops habits and skill. Practice makes perfect? Well, not really—unless your practice is perfect. More accurately, practice makes permanent, so it is wise to make sure you are practicing the right things in the right way. In the end, your commitment to continuous learning by developing your mind, along with your natural talent, is made effective by skill development. You can be the smartest and most talented person in the world, but it doesn't mean a thing if you can't get things done. A leader must commit to self-investment geared toward learning and growth, by practicing the behaviors, and ultimately develop skills around interpersonal relationships, strategic thinking, communicating, and handling conflict. Going back to an earlier point, leadership starts on the inside by identifying who we are and who we wish to become. Then we can focus on the process. How do we get to where we want to go? What is our intended outcome?

Leader, Cultivate Your Competencies

Do you want to be an effective leader? Develop your competencies. Without discrediting technology, we are becoming more robotic and dispassionate in our interactions with one another. Somehow the leader has to break through and connect with his constituents. Communication competencies are crucial. This means not only being able to articulate a clear vision but also clarify values and convictions. Leaders need to become proficient speakers and writers to communicate effectively with others. You need to be clear and concise in delivering your message. Leaders have to know their audience and connect with them. It takes skill and practice. You have to know where you are going before you can lead, but you also have to know and articulate values that define how and why. Being

73

able to envision a future engages the imagination of the mind, both the rational, cognitive part of our mind as well as the passionate, emotional part that springs from convictions and values.

What you say and how you say it matters. Effective communication requires learning the following skills: speaking, writing, reading, and, most importantly, listening. (By the way, we have had formalized classes in all of these areas, but at least in my day, we never had a class in listening.) It was not until I landed my first sales position that I learned about active listening and asking open-ended questions. Listening and asking questions are skills that can be developed with learning and practice. Listening to understand is crucial for any leader and any relationship you wish to have. It means you train yourself to suspend judgment and to focus and not let your internal voices get in the way of listening.

Listening

Hearing is not the same as listening. In fact, you can hear but not actually listen. Case in point: My wife was in the kitchen, and I was in the family room when I heard her talking. At that time, I was also busy reading. Finally, she got my attention by asking, "Did you listen to what I just said?" Ruefully, I had to acknowledge that I heard her but was not actively listening. We have to be attentive and consciously tuned in to be discerning when we listen to what is being said and, for that matter, what is not being said. Often, we get so caught up in what we want to say next that we miss what is being communicated. Our thinking is focused on ourselves, and we miss the point the other person is making.

We also have to watch out for the smooth talkers. These people can sound so convincing that they can lead us to believe and mindlessly accept things that are not necessarily true. We have to pay attention to what is being said and what is not being said. It's like reading a document and missing the fine print. We must be aware that not everyone shares our values and convictions. Some believe in situational ethics, that everything is relative to a situation. "A little lie here and there doesn't matter," they say. Many believe there is no such thing as absolute truth. We must be on guard all the time, or we can be led to believe things that are just not true.

The Habits of the Mind

The competent leader develops habits of the mind. Habits of the mind can easily be ingrained, especially when presented in a pleasing way. Good leaders develop routines that develop into purposeful habits. Elite athletes practice routines that cultivate and ingrain habits that lead to their success. To excel in their performance, they have strictly followed eating, sleep, and exercise habits, not to mention mental conditioning. We should do the same—that is, develop healthy routines that develop into healthy habits. It pays off in the long term.

Recently, I read an opinion article in the *New York Times* that the US spends more than $2 billion on anti-anxiety drugs. According to the report, clinical depression affects about sixteen million people in the US and is estimated to cost the country $210 billion a year in productivity loss. Furthermore, the global revenue for antidepressants is projected to grow to nearly $17 billion by 2020. One of the best ways to manage stress and negativity in your life is to cultivate a healthy mind. Anxiety and depression are different from each other but are linked. Anxiety is the leading mental health issue in the United States. That statement is based on data collected from the national survey of children's health.

We live in the most prosperous and blessed nation on earth, but Americans are some of the most anxious in the world, supported by the results of a world health survey among people from fourteen countries. Americans had significantly higher levels of anxiety than people in Nigeria, Lebanon, and Ukraine. How could this be? Perhaps it could be our culture. Wealth has gotten us to the point where we are plagued with too much stuff and too many options. We get stressed over what we wear, the car we drive, the schools we attend, the food we eat, and the neighborhoods we live in. Our obsession with technology, which is supposed to help us save time, has driven us to micromanage our lives. One message sent to our cell phone, and we feel the need to respond right away! It just increases anxiety all the more.

There are many things driving our anxiety. Could these be related to the decline of faith and moral values? I think so. Unfortunately, our culture has turned away from believing there is such a thing as moral truth. According to George Barna, a renowned pollster, 57 percent of American adults think that knowing what is right and wrong is a matter of personal experience. Millennials, or at least 74 percent of them, agree with the statement. "Whatever is right for your life or works best for you is the only truth you can know" is the prevailing sentiment. It seems we're left either drifting at one extreme or caught in a riptide that is pulling us under at the other extreme. Much of our anxiety comes from habits of the mind that are deep-seated and difficult to change.

> *There are many things driving our anxiety. Could these be related to the decline of faith and moral values?*

Is There Such a Thing as Moral Truth?

It seems to me that we are at a point where "everyone does what is right in his own eyes," as the Bible says in the book of Judges (Judges 21:25). We as a culture and society are in trouble and headed for the worst unless we change this attitude. What brings a sense of security and contentment will not be realized without underpinnings of moral truth. Truth is not a matter of cultural consensus. Many have not given moral truth much thought or any thought, hence people are susceptible to anxiety without even knowing why. Every person with a cognitive ability can look around and know that our world is broken. George Barna reports that many believe that "the highest good is 'finding yourself' and then by living what is right for you." Sad to say, but this is the prevailing mindset in today's culture.

George Barna further defines the morality of self-fulfillment with the following six principles[3]:

> The best way to find yourself is by looking within yourself.
> People should not criticize someone else's life choices.
> To be fulfilled in life, you should pursue the things you desire most.
> The highest goal of life is to enjoy it as much as possible.
> People can believe whatever they want, as long as those beliefs don't affect society.
> Any kind of sexual expression between two consenting adults is acceptable.

On the surface, some of these principles may have some merit, but these principles are very self-focused. A culture that is dominated by a me-my-and-mine mentality does not bode well! As leaders, we have to stand up for convictions of truth and lead others to the truth and to a change of heart and mind.

The good news is that redemption is possible no matter how far we have fallen. First, it does require a change in worldview from self-fulfillment to helping people think about moral truth. We all are subjects to our Creator, and He has given the blueprint for morality. When we make a choice to acknowledge our brokenness, repent, commit our lives to Christ, and place our faith and trust in Him, a profound thing happens. The Spirit of God works in us, and we become open to change—primarily because we change from the inside out, and our worldview changes. And now, being subjects to King of kings, we have access to God, who can help us transform. We will start to see ourselves as we really are, and the Spirit of God begins to make changes in our lives because now our lives are not about self-fulfillment but fulfillment in Him, which plays out in service to others. David Kinnaman and Gabe Lyons, in their book, define the six principles of God's moral order:

---

[3] You can get deeper into these principles by reading *Good Faith: Being a Christian When Society Thinks You're Irrelevant and Extreme*, a book by David Kinnaman and Gabe Lyons and published by Baker Books.

To find yourself, discover the truth outside yourself, in Jesus.

Loving others does not always mean staying silent.

Joy is not found in pursuing our own desires but in giving ourselves to bless others.

The highest goal of life is giving glory to God.

God gives people the freedom to believe whatever they want, but those beliefs always affect society.

God designed boundaries for sex and sexuality in order for humans to flourish.

Contrast the six principles of God's moral order with the previously mentioned six principles of morality of self-fulfillment. Notice how different they are in terms of focus?

Everything we endeavor to accomplish begins with the first step. Change is seldom easy, and changing who we are is even more difficult. To be self-aware of our sinful nature, our minds and our hearts have to be tuned in to our conscience and what we know and believe. Our beliefs, over time and with resistance to temptation, forge into convictions. Eventually, with the right action and behavior, habits of the mind are changed as we begin to think differently. As leaders, our mindset changes from principles that lead to serve us to genuine service to others, where the focus is helping the ones we are called to lead. To quote my friend James Jackson, "Leaders grow from motivation of self to motivation of many." Change requires examining our lives in the moment. When we are humbled to welcome the spirit of God to engage to the inner core of our lives, we will be open to be changed. The change *to* our life happens instantly when we acknowledge and repent of the sin in our life; the change *in* our life happens over time by being obedient to the Word of God. There is good and there is evil in the world. We know evil when we see it and experience the destruction that evil brings. As bad as evil is, paradoxically, when we think about it, without evil, how could we know what is good?

What Now?

While we reflect on what we did during the day, we should take inventory of our thoughts and actions. Do you like putting your thoughts on paper (or typing them out on your computer)? Try journaling. It is a good and practical way to bring awareness of our daily time investments. Making lists is another way. Reflecting and being attentive to our thoughts and actions requires time set aside for introspection. We usually know good habits from bad, but some can be subtle. Fortunately, if we work hard to cultivate good habits and put them into practice, we can crowd out bad habits. We must be vigilant, for even the most experienced leaders can fall prey to bad habits. As I end this chapter, let me underscore the need to develop competence in the following areas:

- *Having a mindset of personal responsibility* for personal growth and development as well as responsibility for the well-being of others, society, and the culture at large.
- *Discovering how to learn.* We all have different ways of learning. Some are naturally good listeners and are better than others in this aspect, but a good leader needs to build skills around listening. Leaders must be active readers, although some are better at learning from reading than others. Some learn best by doing, but we all learn by taking action. For deeper insight, I recommend Peter Drucker's *Thoughts on Managing Oneself.* My point is that leaders must constantly be learning. Learn to listen well, write well, and speak well.
- *Identifying values and cultivating moral convictions and searching for truth.* Fundamentally, the leader must think about and establish beliefs about the following questions: Who am I? What do I believe? Why do I believe? Why is it important? What are my values and convictions? Where am I going? How will I get there?
- *Finding a purpose.* Where will you make your contribution for the betterment of society? Many of us fall into our life's work.

It can be difficult, especially for young people, to identify their unique calling in life. One discovers it through paying close attention to one's life experiences, self-reflection, and self-awareness. Some never find it, and the reward for their labor is mere existence. We must actively search for what we can be passionate about and be alert, active, and patient at the same time. In the big picture, our purpose is to glorify our Creator, but I also believe each of us is created for a specific purpose, where we can make our unique contribution.

- *Creating an environment of optimism and hope.* Hope is always future focused, and a good leader leads with optimism and hope, sometimes in the midst of discouragement and despair. The leader must be able to articulate a vision that brings hope for followers, and that can be a difficult task. It is what made Winston Churchill such a powerful leader during World War II. Winston Churchill's biggest legacy was his steadfast encouragement to Great Britain during the harrowing times of World War II. In the end, a leader must encourage his followers.
- *Building teams and accomplishing goals through the help of other people.* Gaining alignment and building teams that work is a challenge but something every leader has to accomplish. The engagement of others is brought about by transparency, authenticity, shared values, clearly articulated goals, compassion ... and a sense of humor. (You need to be able to laugh with other people too!)
- *Innovating and keeping pace with the changes in technology.* If a leader does not look for ways to innovate and change, the company will die. The leader must always be challenging the process and embed that mindset into the culture.

Competence—without it, leadership fails.

CHAPTER 9

CONVICTION

"What is the difference between values and convictions?"

I'm often asked this question. Let me tell you how I usually reply. Values are standards. They can be aspirational, but they are not always concrete. We have values that shift over time. For example, some things I valued in my twenties or thirties are different from what I value today. Values are important because they help guide our decisions and actions or behaviors relative to our situation or season in life. (But please note that I do not mean to imply that values are constantly changing.)

Moral truth and ethics align more with convictions. Convictions are deeper and are anchored in our beliefs. We are not as apt to compromise on our convictions. Leadership requires strong convictions because sooner or later you will be tested. Maybe not in the face of a life-threatening situation, but as a leader, you will have to make difficult decisions and choices. You will either be loved or hated for them. But when you think about it, could anyone really stand up for a cause they believe in, especially when facing violence or death threats, without convictions? Simply put, conviction is leadership put into action.

Tension with Science

What if we believe and are convicted of something we cannot scientifically prove? As a Christian, I have convictions related to my faith that will not change. In fact, they grow deeper as I learn and practice what I believe to be true. It doesn't always win me friends, but without real beliefs and convictions, life would be shallow and superficial. Our convictions govern our behaviors and our attitudes. Values are important, but convictions are more visceral in nature and are much less likely to be compromised. Convictions are tied what we know to be true based not just on feelings. Convictions are born out of objective truth about what we believe and is the source of passion for the leader. Unfortunately, we can also have convictions about what we believe that is not truth. Values are formed more by the external things. Convictions are driven internally by what we believe so strongly that we refuse to compromise. Motivation of the heart is key. As leaders, we must remember our ultimate end. All the great leaders of the past come to the same ending. Their legacy lives on only by the convictions they leave behind and their successors carry on.

The kind of leaders that move people and inspire them to act are motivated by a passion generated by their beliefs and convictions. But not all convictions are good. For instance, the internal core of a leader could be void of moral truth, and what they believe could be self-focused, based on a lust for power or ideologies that come and go. Many strong organizations have fallen because convictions are based on false ideologies or convictions are weak and do not hold up under pressure. Success sometimes can foster a false sense of security, and we can coast and let convictions wane and achievement spiral down. This can happen to a person, an organization, or even a country.

Lessons from History

We should learn lessons from history about what is good and what is evil. Nazism threatened all of Europe but in the end was exposed and defeated. Remember, it is possible to have convictions and be passionate about false beliefs. Sadly, we can be blinded by emotions and swayed by our fallible reasoning. Despite good people's best intentions, if not careful, they can still be taken in. Not everyone in

Germany was taken in by Hitler's hideous ideology, but many were and followed his leadership. Leaders who are passionate about what they believe move others to act. This gives us another reason why we must set our convictions on moral truth.

If our convictions are based on moral truth, we will be less likely to be sucked into false ideologies. It makes all the difference in the world. There is much carnage in the pages of history that has been created by corrupt and evil leaders. Conversely, there have been great turning points in history where the destinies of nations have been shaped by noble leaders with deep, unwavering convictions. We've talked about two such leaders, Abraham Lincoln and William Wilberforce. On the other hand, there are also evil leaders in the likes of Adolf Hitler and Joseph Stalin.

By nature, we have a tendency to follow our own rules. We chafe at the thought of being accountable to constraints against doing whatever we want. Leaders with conviction have to be clear about what they believe and their source of truth. Al Mohler, in his book *Convicted to Lead*, says, "At the center of the true leader's heart and mind you will find convictions that drive and determine everything else." Again, convictions are beliefs that we are willing to live and die for.

Convictions are what drive us and give us unwavering focus. Leaders with conviction stir people up from the inside out to move forward and overcome roadblocks they might encounter along the way. Convictions are seen and experienced when a leader stands in the face of threats, ridicule, and persecution and does not back down.

In my experience, when asking others about their convictions, I often get a blank stare. Many have not thought deeply about convictions. Without convictions, we are like a sailboat without a keel, easily blown in the direction of the wind. Convictions should be like the keel on a sailboat. It will

Are you willing to sacrifice or die for your convictions?

stabilize us, allow us to move forward and stay on course, and prevent us from drifting in the wrong direction.

What Shapes Our Convictions?

To determine one's convictions takes work, time, and a devotion to learning what is truth. Our convictions are shaped by experiential knowledge and what we have learned from a number of sources— our parents, our places of worship, teachers, coaches, friends, and good books. Clarity and courage of our convictions come mostly from conscious thinking and reflection and the hard work of understanding ourselves and the world around us. This is where our worldview comes into play. The cultural worldview is secular, where self is at the center and where truth and values are determined. A secularist views a Christian worldview as a personal belief system, a private matter not relevant to science. In other words, keep your views about Christianity to yourself. A secularist chooses not to believe in God. From a secularist view, if you choose to believe in the God of creation and truth, your views are irrelevant and you should keep your beliefs to yourself.

So, how do we know if our convictions are right? Society is making it easy to blur the line between what is right and what is wrong. We live in an environment that has been broken into factions. Our motives are flawed when we believe we are right based on feelings that justify devaluing others who don't subscribe to the prevailing ideology where we may be aligned—or not. If we don't agree with what is espoused as enlightened thought, we are labeled as intolerant or worse.

Conviction Defined

So in the midst of this conflict of beliefs, how do we determine convictions? Steven Stosny, founder of CompassionPower, defines conviction, "Conviction is the strong belief that a behavior is right, moral and consistent with your deeper values. It offers a kind of certainty, not about the world, but about the morality of your own behavior." He clarifies further by saying this:

The best way to know that you're acting out of conviction and not resentment or arrogance (based on a feeling of certainty), is to state why your behavior is right and moral. If your answer has conviction, it will embody your deeper values. If it's resentful or arrogant, it will devalue someone else.

He makes some good points, but I would add that you need a source for what is moral truth, and it won't be found in how we feel about something or what someone rationalizes as truth. Truth is not synonymous with feelings or, for that matter, intellectual arrogance and pride.

The leader today faces the daunting task of bringing into alignment people of diverse beliefs and backgrounds. The leader needs to clarify his or her own convictions by thinking about right and wrong, what is good and moral, and what is not. A leader's task is to shape thinking and influence behaviors that will lead to accomplishment. It is not easy when our culture has been segmented into factions that tend to divide and pit us against one another. It's as difficult as walking on a tightrope, trying to be politically correct in everything to avoid conflict and being accused of offending. But trying to appease everybody satisfies no one. In today's world, the leader has to remove the labels that have such a damaging impact on our society for the accomplishment of common good. What is needed is both love and respect for every person. This, however, doesn't mean that everybody has to agree on everything. In fact, that would not be good. To fight for a cause and to fulfill a vision, there has to be, from the leader, love and respect for every person. Again, this should stem from a conviction that we are all created in the image of God.

When asked which is the great commandment, Jesus answered this way in Mark 12:30–31:

And you shall love the Lord your God with all your heart and with all your soul and with all your mind and with all your strength. The second is this: "You shall love your neighbor as yourself."

For more insight, read the parable of the Good Samaritan in Luke 10:25–37. Jesus did not seek to segment the Jews from the Samaritans even though Samaritans were despised by the Jewish people.

We are fortunate, so far, to live in a free and open society in our country. In other parts of the world, there are those whose freedom is taken away, and governments and various institutions try to choose special interest groups by closing down dissenting debate. We all have the freedom to believe what we choose, and we should be willing to live with the consequences of our choices. Sometimes we will be subject to ridicule and harassment for standing up for our convictions. In the end, leaders have to know what they believe, know why they believe it and why it is important, and then live and model what their convictions dictate.

The Power of Conviction

Steve Jobs believed that the personal computer could change individual lives. He had a vision that everyone should have a personal computer in their home. I mean, he really believed it! He once said, "Being the richest man in the cemetery doesn't matter to me. Going to bed at night saying we've done something wonderful, that's what matters to me." When Jobs was trying to persuade John Sculley to join Apple, he asked, "Do you want to sell sugar water for the rest of your life or do you want to come with me to change the world?" His convictions were contagious to those around him, and that is the mission of a leader. He also said, "Technology is nothing. What is important is that you have faith in people, that they are basically good and smart, and if you give them the tools, they'll do wonderful things with them." It is true that without people, there is no leadership. While I agree with Jobs's statement about people, it must be the right people. Not everyone fit into Apple's culture. In fact, John Sculley and Steve Jobs experienced conflicts that led to Jobs leaving Apple. When John Sculley exited the company, Steve Jobs returned and led Apple to even greater heights.

Select the Right People

Along with having a well-conceived and articulated vision, the leader must also have the ability to select the right people. A good leader surrounds themselves with team members whose beliefs and convictions are in alignment. Generally speaking, people want to be part of something bigger than themselves. When convictions of a leader run deep and are genuinely conveyed with enthusiasm, it spreads like wildfire. A leader's conviction has to be sustainable, having more than a burst of energy—a long-lasting passion that will overcome difficulty, temporary roadblocks and find a way to innovate and succeed. This doesn't mean surrounding yourself with people who agree with everything you say. Constructive conflict is healthy when it is focused on different points of view and stays away from personal attacks and disparagement. Knowing the why is most important. You should be able to answer why you all are doing what you are doing. What and how we achieve is guided by the leader but implemented by the people.

Always remember that convictions run deep! They are sourced from our inner core. Are you willing to sacrifice or die for your convictions? Convictions are linked to our intense commitment that raises our level of passion and energy and drives us to achieve and excel. Our beliefs, values, and convictions anchor our character. Convictions tie our very souls to truth and serve as the bedrock that holds a leader steadfast in difficult times and when tempted to compromise.

Making an impact and having influence in people's lives, their companies, and other enterprises operating in the workplace is the leader's ultimate task. Moral virtues like integrity, justice, fairness, and compassion, along with the ability to relate authentically to the needs of those whom they lead, define a good leader. The drive for learning and growing must never cease but must be governed by humility and the avoidance of intellectual arrogance. Leadership is an inside-out job. It begins within but manifests outward to serving others by respecting them, loving them, and leading them to change and grow.

CHAPTER 10

COURAGE

Courage is an overarching characteristic of everything we have talked about. Courage defines character, enables competence, and is the power of conviction. Courage provides us the strength to stand up for justice and honest principles, to be open to learn from others and from our mistakes, and to love one another. What is courage? Why do we need it? It's no wonder the ancient Greeks thought courage was the "master virtue, because without courage, you would never use your other virtues.

Courage versus Fear

Is courage being reckless? No, it's not about taking outlandish risks or not being fearful of anything. We are, after all, wired to be emotional creatures, so it is quite natural to feel distress, anxiety, and fear. Fear can save us from harm. The problem is when these emotions take over and control what we think and do. When strong emotions like fear and anger take over, we are prone to making poor choices and bad decisions. It is thinking and acting with a sound mind and courage that enables us to move through times of distress and fear. Sometimes we think our courage comes from leaning on our self-awareness and

Don't let fear stop you from making your unique contribution as a person and as a leader.

self-control. There is something to be said for being self-aware and practicing self-control, but self-reliance is not the main source of courage. Our ability to act courageously is sourced from our faith and convictions and our most powerful force, love. In Colossians 3:12–14, the apostle Paul gave this advice to the Colossians that we can still use today:

> Put on then as God's chosen ones … compassion, kindness, humility, meekness, and patience, bearing with one another and if one has a complaint against another, forgiving each other as the Lord has forgiven you, you must also forgive … and above all put on love which binds everything in perfect harmony.

As a leader, you are going to face frightening circumstances, but you do not have to be controlled by fear. A courageous response may be difficult, but take a deep breath and realize that your situation is not hopeless. You can take action with faith and conviction to bring your emotions under control as long as you know what you believe and why you believe it. Why is it that we can recognize the potential in others who are held back by fear but miss it in ourselves?

So much of what we could do to make our unique contribution does not get done because we hold back in fear—fear of failure, fear of what others might think, fear of knowing the facts, fear of facing reality. We fear for our kids, how they will fare in the tumultuous, unstable world we live in. There are other fears that plague us, things we can't control, like fear of a bad economy, a downturn in business, the health of our finances—the list could go on and on. As we said, fear is a very powerful emotion that has the power to control us. Fear brings on worry and anxiety, which damages our physical, mental, emotional, and spiritual health. As we said before, our fears many times trace back to the way we think, patterns of thinking that have been engraved over time. Our thinking and our emotions are inextricably linked.

Fear versus Reality

One funny thing about fear is that much of what we fear often never materializes. I don't mean to minimize the reality of feeling fear, for it is natural. But we need to understand that fear can cause you to avoid things you should do and, conversely, cause you to do things you wouldn't normally do. For example, you know you should stand up for convictions but end up shrinking back because of what others might think or say. On the other hand, you may charge into a burning building, risking your life, if you know someone is inside and could be rescued. The difference between these two examples is the object of our focus. When we are fearful to stand up for our convictions, the focus is on ourselves. When we rush into a burning building, we do so because we fear for the safety of others. This time, the focus is not on us but on others.

The Conscientious Objector

Desmond Doss had conviction and courage. Drafted into the US Army during World War II, he was mocked and ostracized by his drill instructor and fellow soldiers because of his convictions. A conscientious objector, he believed that he could not kill another human being. Desmond would not even carry a rifle. He became a medic but was ridiculed constantly and was accused of being a coward. Eventually, he ended up on the battlefront on the island of Okinawa. As Desmond's unit moved from a landing on the beach to make their way up the cliffs, the Japanese attacked his unit, who had just made it to the top. A brutal battle was waged, and many soldiers died, and many were severely wounded.

In the midst of the attack, Desmond went to work and made a makeshift stretcher and began running from body to body, rescuing the wounded and lowering them down to the beach below with a combination of ropes and pulleys. It was reported that he even rescued some of the enemy combatants! Barraged with a constant hail of bullets flying around him, Desmond ran from foxhole to foxhole, rescuing soldiers from his unit, one at a time, lowering each man to the relative safety of the beach. He became a hero with his unit. Desmond Doss a coward? Hardly. Later, he was awarded the Medal of Honor from President Truman for saving seventy-five men. His story was recently told in the movie *Hacksaw Ridge*. Desmond's convictions would be merely words if he had not acted with courage. You could also say that without his convictions, he would not have acted so courageously.

Not many of us get tested on a literal battlefield like Desmond, but if you step up to the mantle of leadership, you will be tested. Rick Warren, in his book *The Purpose-Driven Life*, says, "Life is a test, life is a trust, and life is a temporary assignment." What do you want to be a measure of your life? It is not wise to try to be or do something stupid to prove your courage. But don't let fear stop you from making your unique contribution as a person and a leader. The book of Proverbs gives us some good advice. Proverbs 22:3 says, "The prudent sees danger and hides himself, but the simple go on and suffer for it." Be courageous but make good decisions!

Speaking in Public and Other Fears

Would you rather die than speak in public? You are not alone. Fear of public speaking has been found to be a more pressing concern than death, according to a ranking of society's most pervasive fears. You may laugh, but as a young leader, I remember all too well my heart pounding, my mouth dry, and my face flushed in my first experience of public speaking—or, for that matter, my second, third, and fourth. I still get butterflies in my stomach when called upon to speak in front of a group. Someone once said that the trick is to get those butterflies flying in formation. Also, I have realized that a little nervous energy gets adrenaline flowing and gives you more energy in front of a group. As a leader, public speaking is a competence that needs to be mastered, and it requires courage. It doesn't hurt to get training. For me, it was Dale Carnegie.

Courage can be put into practice in many ways, like stepping out of our comfort zone. We already talked about public speaking. You can start training yourself to overcome your fear of public speaking by taking small steps. Start by learning how to introduce yourself to a stranger. Remember to ask open-ended questions. And listen! Put your focus on the other person. Be curious. Start speaking up in low-risk situations. Every step you take toward courage builds personal strength and character. Look for ways to purposefully step out of your comfort zone, for when we are out of our comfort zone, we learn, we grow in confidence, and we gain courage.

We cannot be an effective leader and lack courage. Many times, we react out of fear instead of acting out of faith. Fear is a natural emotion and prepares us for flight or fight. But courage is bringing fear under control and taking action by moving through it. Building courage leads to confidence. The word *confidence* is sourced from the Latin word *confidere,* meaning "to have full trust or walking in faith." Standing up for our convictions may not line up with what is politically correct. It certainly takes courage and confidence. Act out of faith; don't react out of fear.

> *Act out of faith; don't react out of fear.*

People of Faith Are People of Courage

> But the fruit of the Spirit is love, joy, peace, patience, kindness, goodness, faithfulness, gentleness and self-control. (Galatians 5:22)

Don't we wish everyone had all these attributes? We have focused on courage, but the fuel for courage can be summed up in one word: love. As a leader, we have to care about those we lead. The spirit of courage and the spirit of love go hand in hand. Love is others focused, while fear is self-focused.

The greatest example we have of love is Jesus Christ, who gave His life for us. In fact, when a lawyer challenged Jesus by asking which is the great commandment, Jesus answered, "You shall love the Lord your God with all your heart, soul and with all your mind. This is the first and greatest commandment. And a second is like it: You shall love your neighbor as yourself" (Matthew 22:37–29). The order is clear: first, love God, then others, and then yourself.

The Builder of the Wall

In the book of Nehemiah, we can read another story of effective leadership. Nehemiah lived up to the four attributes of leadership—character, competence, conviction, and courage. But who was he and what did he do?

Nehemiah, an Israelite, was exiled in Persia. As the story begins, Nehemiah is serving as a cupbearer to King Artaxerxes. It was a position of stature and influence. For a foreigner and exile to gain such a position was extraordinary. First, he had to earn the trust of the king. Second, he had to be knowledgeable about the culture and protocol. Third, he must have lived an exemplary life. It was quite an achievement to be an outsider and gain a prestigious and privileged position. A cupbearer was more than a butler. He was in the presence of the king and interacted with the king on a daily basis and could be of influence in many ways. It was a cushy job and one that offered a measure of security. Nehemiah was in a much better position than many of his fellow displaced Israelites and certainly better off than the Israelites back in his homeland.

Bad News about Jerusalem

One day, his brother Hanani, traveling from Jerusalem, met with Nehemiah. Nehemiah inquired about the people who were back in his homeland and the city he loved. He found that the people were struggling to survive. His beloved city of Jerusalem was in shambles. Hanani reported, "The wall of Jerusalem is broken down, and the gates are destroyed by fire." As soon as Nehemiah heard the news, he broke down and mourned for days. Nehemiah loved his people, he loved the city of Jerusalem and his heritage, and he felt compelled to do something. He prayed, fasted, and reflected for days.

He needed to talk to the king, but when you approach the king, it can be a dicey situation. The king has the power to decide your fate and order your execution. The king wanted everyone to be upbeat and serve him joyfully. But Nehemiah couldn't hide his sadness. King Artaxerxes picked up on it and asked, "Why is your face sad, seeing you are not sick? This is nothing but sadness of heart." Nehemiah was scared but nevertheless told the king what was troubling his heart. He said, "The city, the place of my father's grave, lies in ruins, and its gates have been destroyed by fire." The king then asked what he wanted to happen, and Nehemiah made an audacious request. Boldly, Nehemiah said, "Allow me to go back and rebuild the city." The king responded with more questions: "How long will it take? When will you return?" Nehemiah was ready for his questions and answered them all. He stuck his neck out even further by asking the king for letters to grant him authority and also for resources to rebuild the walls and gates. Finally, he asked for travel protection to make the journey.

Nehemiah acted like a strong leader when he pushed himself beyond his comfort zone.

Nehemiah acted like a strong leader when he pushed himself beyond his comfort zone. In his heart, he was convicted that he could do something to rebuild Jerusalem, and he was motivated by his love for his people, who were living in despair. He courageously took action, and the king granted his request.

Rebuilding the Wall

When Nehemiah arrived at Jerusalem, he did not start issuing commands or acting like he was in command. Instead, he kept his mission to himself for a time. He was low-key and went out under the cover of darkness to access the problem. He gathered the facts before he made his plan to share with the people. After days of assessment and planning, he was ready to communicate the problem and his vision. As he addressed the people, he described the problem and brought the people into alignment with his vision for rebuilding. He challenged them with, "Come let us build the wall of Jerusalem, that we may no longer suffer derision." His words were "we" and "us," not "I" and "me." Nehemiah engaged the people and encouraged them to take action. No leader gets things done by themselves.

As they started building, they were being harassed and ridiculed by those who were opposed to the rebuilding of the city. Always expect opposition to change, especially when it interrupts the status quo. There were many who were taking advantage of the beaten-down, discouraged people. However, with the mission and vision clear, everyone, including the priests, rolled up their sleeves and worked. Nehemiah had given them hope. The ridicule and mockery continued, but the people ignored them. But, as often happens when verbal attacks fail to achieve the results the opposition wants, they step up to threats of physical attacks. So, as good leaders often do, Nehemiah made adjustments to the plan to counter the threats of physical harm. He placed the workers strategically, with half of the workers building the wall and the other half armed with swords to guard the builders laying stones to build the wall. In spite of opposition and threats, the walls and gates were completed in fifty-two days. What a remarkable feat!

Lessons from Nehemiah's Leadership

What can we learn from Nehemiah's leadership? Here are some key points:

Nehemiah's character was developed over a long time of service to the king, and when a big moment of leadership was presented, he was ready. He was humble and did not act impulsively. He was moved when he received the news of the city in shambles and the people struggling to survive. He prayed and reflected on the facts that he heard and made a choice to act. The way he lived his life had earned the trust of the king and was seen in a favorable light when he approached King Artaxerxes. It was a moment of courage. He later quickly earned the trust and respect of most of his people in Jerusalem. Nehemiah left a comfortable lifestyle to devote himself to the work of rebuilding the city. He was motivated by his love for God, his love for the people, and his love for the city of Jerusalem. Nehemiah did not think of his own comfort and well-being but accepted the mantle of leadership and responsibility for a calling beyond himself. The lesson for us is to be intentional about developing our character.

Nehemiah, over time, had developed a number of competencies. He was an effective communicator, a thinker, a strategist, and a planner. He paid close attention to detail. It is a good lesson to learn when we dedicate ourselves to the task at hand. Everything we do—the choices and decisions we make—is preparation for the future. We never know when a call to lead may come. Leaders are always learning through experience and by reading and listening to others. All that Nehemiah had done in the past had prepared him for this moment. We never know when opportunity to lead will present itself. Whatever you do, do it wholeheartedly, because what you do and how you do it will prepare you for what comes next. Be purposeful in gaining competency.

Every tangible thing we have accumulated in life is temporary. What we believe in to the point of conviction is lasting. Nehemiah's convictions were embedded in his faith. He was convicted that the city of Jerusalem needed to be rebuilt to honor his God and to protect the Jewish people who had returned from exile. Nehemiah left his privileged position in serving the king to a difficult and risky task of rebuilding a city where he faced threatening opposition. In the midst of rebuilding the wall, Nehemiah took action to stop the oppression of the poor. He restored ownership of their fields and vineyards, eliminated the burden of high interest rates, and gave generously from his own resources. He placed people in leadership positions, taught them, and established order. All that Nehemiah accomplished was born out of his conviction to step out and act on his call to lead.

All of what Nehemiah accomplished came from acting out of courage and not reacting out of fear. His character, competence, conviction, and courage yielded a credibility that enabled Nehemiah to gain the trust of his followers. He acted with courage. His constituents followed with courage. Courage initiates action. To quote Albert Moeller, "True credibility rests in the ability of others to trust what the leader can do." Ultimately, Nehemiah left behind a great legacy of his service to his God and his people. His story is one that has lasted that we can read about and learn from to this day. The ultimate goal of a leader is to leave a legacy that impacts and influences the generations that follow. Nehemiah's story is one of many chronicled in the Bible, and today we can still learn from his legacy.

Fear prevents many people from living the life they were meant to live. That's why a vision must be a picture of what could be in the future of your life. Think ten years from now. "Play the tape forward," as John Townsend says in his book, *Eight Things You Must Do*. It is the vision and hope we have that will help spur us on and overcome obstacles that will surely come our way. The reality of life is that nothing happens exactly as we plan. There will be unexpected tests and trials that will shape our lives. Some will be brought on by choices and decisions we make. Some trials will be brought on by circumstances that are completely out of our control. Charles Swindoll said, "I am convinced that life is 10% what happens to me and 90% of how I react to it. And so it is with you … we are in charge of our attitudes." In most cases, the only thing you can control is yourself and how you choose to think and act.

Leadership requires stepping up and embracing leadership opportunities, but it also demands the courage to look within and be willing to face our character and flaws and adjust accordingly. It is never too late to recognize a turning point in our lives and change our behavior for the better. And it always takes courage to make this happen.

CHAPTER 11

LEADERSHIP ROLES

There is a cry for strong leadership in all areas of our society. In this chapter, we'll be exploring the kind of leadership needed in a number of areas. Let's start with the most basic of all—leadership in the family. The greatest need for strong leadership starts in the home. The family is the primary building block of civilization, and today, too many family units are fractured and broken. The result is far-reaching. The breakup of families strikes at the core of our communities and weakens the strength of our country. What does leadership look like in the relationship between husband and wife, and between parents and children?

Leadership in the Home

In Husband-Wife Relationship

Many couples go through difficult periods in their marriage. If it was easy, we wouldn't value the relationship, nor would we learn that love is much more than feeling. When we're focused only on how we feel, we fail to consider the needs of the other person. God meant for marriage to be the foundation for civilization, to build a society and culture where we learn personal sacrifice and serving. It is within the context of marriage where we learn to disagree and to put aside selfish ambition and not measure everything by how it makes us feel. We learn about self-control and controlling the tongue. To quote Dallas Willard,

> Many families break up not because of physical abuse and infidelity, the marriage is destroyed with constant criticism, biting remarks, cold indifference, sarcasm, putting each other down, and constantly seeking to have it your own way. Because experiencing personal gratification and personal fulfillment is a paramount value of our culture we are unsatisfied when lifestyle ambitions cannot be realized when financial resources are short ... then patience wears thin and families break up because we deserve better. All of it is putting "the self" at the center.

For many of us, marriage is our first call to a meaningful leadership position. From a biblical point of view, when a man gets married and has children, he automatically assumes the responsibility for his family. Leadership is not optional; it's mandatory. Up to now, a crucial part of character development that we have not focused on is love and what it means to love. Love is a powerful force even outside the context of being a Christian. Genuine love is a gift from God. In fact, the Bible says in 1 John 4:7, "Beloved let us love one another for love is from God." Love is first a state of being before it becomes an action. In other words, it starts from inside of us and then flows out to others.

So, what does love look like within the covenant of marriage? How does love relate to leadership? First let's look at how 1 Corinthians 13:1–13, one the greatest passages of scripture, spells out what love is:

> If I speak in tongues of men and of angels, but have not love, I am a noisy gong or a clanging cymbal. And if I have prophetic powers and understand all mysteries and all knowledge, and if I have faith, so as to remove mountains, but have not love I am nothing.

If I give away all I have and deliver up my body to be burned, but have not love I gain nothing.

Love is patient and kind, love does not envy or boast; it is not arrogant or rude. It does not insist on its own way; it is not irritable or resentful; it does not rejoice at wrongdoing but rejoices in truth. Love bears all things, believes all things, hopes all things, endures all things. Love never ends, as for prophecies they will pass away; as for tongues they will cease; as for knowledge, it will pass away. For we know now in part and we prophesy in part, but when the perfect comes, the partial will pass away. When I was a child I spoke as a child, I thought like a child, I reasoned like a child. When I became a man, I gave up childish ways. For now we see in a mirror dimly but then face to face. Now I know in part; then I shall know fully, even as I have been fully known. So now faith, hope and love abide, these three; but the greatest of these is love.

Love is about the motivation of the heart. It is our state of being and not just a feeling or sensation. When we learn to love God and love others, we are conditioning our heart for good. And the heart is where choices are made, both good and bad. It works not only for leadership in the family but also in leadership in our vocations, in our churches, and in our communities.

In Parent-Child Relationship

It starts with an attitude of our culture that has become laissez-faire, dismissing the importance and the covenant relationship of marriage. Because of the decay in our morals and the availability of divorce laws, it's now easy to terminate the covenant vows of marriage and walk away from the sacrifice and hard work of building and leading a family. The collateral damage of the breakup of the nuclear family causes hurt and pain not only to the children but to the extended family and even friendships. There are circumstances where divorce is the only recourse, when the safety and welfare of a wife or children are at stake, or perhaps when infidelity is involved. Most divorces, however, are caused by failures in leadership. Problems in the relationship are not resolved and continue to fester until everything blows up. This is an area I am passionate about because of the failure of my first marriage. The deleterious effect on my family is easy to see in hindsight. We can be forgiven for our past mistakes and work hard to restore broken lives, but that does not mean consequences magically disappear. There is a reason the Bible tells us that God hates divorce.

This is hard for me to write because I gave up on my own marriage after being married for fifteen years. But the reality is I didn't know how to be married. Divorce is a big problem, especially if there are children. The wounds of divorce are devastating, and the children also bear the scars that last a lifetime. Children often cope by drawing inward or by striking out. Even though some have tried for a "friendly divorce (which is probably better than the alternative, a hostile divorce), the fact remains that neither can be as good a parent apart as they are together. In a recent *Wall Street Journal* article, a woman who went through a friendly divorce said that she has yet to meet someone who says they are as good parents separated as they were together. Also, divorce often leads to another marriage that brings its own set of challenges with blended families. In addition, while roughly 50 percent of marriages end in divorce, second marriage divorce rates are even higher at over 60 percent. As a result, many children watch and experience their parents go through not one but two divorces.

But the problem isn't divorce per se (as in my case, in my previous marriage). As I've mentioned, I didn't know how to be married or how to lead. Dallas Willard addresses this issue in his book, *Renovation of the Heart*. He puts it this way:

> The problem is that people don't know how to be married. They don't actually get married in many

cases, though they go through a legal and possibly a religious ceremony. They are, sad to say, incapable of marriage, the kind of constant mutual blessing that can make two people in conjugal relation literally one whole person.

He continues:

Anyone who wishes to really understand the situation with divorce and family breakup today should begin with careful study of the giving of one's self and the receiving of another as manifested in the vows of this traditional service: "I, take thee, to have and to hold from this day forward, for better or for worse, for richer or poorer, in sickness and in health, to love and to cherish, till death do us part." Insight into the meaning of these vows will clearly bring out why the ideal intent of marriage is one man and one woman for life. The mutual submission to each other in awe of the Lord.

I am grateful that God has restored my relationships with my children and that Barbara, my second wife, and I have now been married thirty-nine years. God's grace and forgiveness are truly amazing, but consequences and scars remain.

Today, more and more young people are just moving in together, thinking they can "see if it works before committing to each other in marriage. This attitude may be born out of what they have all too often have seen or experienced in their own families. Too often, these arrangements fall apart because there is no real commitment. Often, a baby is born and ends up being raised by a single parent or passed back and forth, thereby losing the security and stability of having a father and mother working together to solve relational issues. The percentage of divorces among those who live together before marriage is greater than for those who don't. This proves the point that living together before committing to marriage doesn't guarantee a successful marriage.

Leadership in Our Churches

Many churches are dying, especially in the once-strong mainstream denominations. Why? Because leadership is absent, and the truth of the Gospel has been watered down. Our culture is shaping our churches instead of our churches shaping the culture. More and more, the message of a"feel-good, loving God is promoted, limiting the power of the Creator, minimizing the Fall of humankind, and focusing more on how we feel versus God's intolerance of sin and the consequences of disobeying Him. The good news is that God does love us. This, however, doesn't mean that we can do whatever seems right in our own eyes and continue to ignore God. There will always be a price to pay.

Leadership failures in the church have devastating consequences too. We hear reports about child abuse, acts of immorality, and mishandling of money, among others. Churches have become places of entertainment and pop psychology rather than where God's unadulterated truth is preached. Some pastors have become celebrities instead of servants of God, proclaiming a partial truth and proclaiming that God will grant us health, wealth, and solution to all our problems.

What is desperately needed is leadership not just in the top positions in the church but at every level. The senior leaders in our churches, the pastors, have the responsibility of teaching and equipping believers to go out in the world and bring the light of the Gospel into their vocational roles, family lives, and communities. We are not to sit in the pews as passive receivers of the Word but doers of the Word. Our churches should be the major force in shaping

Some churches have become places of entertainment and pop psychology rather than where God's unadulterated truth is preached.

our culture, contrary to the belief that education and politics are the answer. Change starts at the individual soul level, where the redeemed people of God are equipped with character, competence, conviction, and courage to change the course of our broken world.

Leadership in Our Schools

Our schools have taken over the cultivation of the minds and hearts of our children. I'm not trying to imply that all teachers are trying to indoctrinate our kids, especially in their younger years. Nonetheless, laws are being passed to take any teaching of God out of the classroom and introduce ideologies that are contrary to Judeo-Christian values. At the college and university levels, the administrators and teachers are even more blatant about purging God from campuses. University professors are mocking the Christian worldview and shut down any student who takes a contrary position. Moral truth and belief in God are being mocked in many of the classrooms of our universities. Leading change at school is going to be difficult. Young adults between the ages of eighteen and thirty make important decisions that set the course of their entire life. Unfortunately, many young people return home from college stripped of their faith in God and the Bible.

Beyond our school classrooms is the bureaucracy of our education system where governance and curriculum is determined. The void in moral leadership is apparent based on textbooks that change historical facts and with mandates handed down to accommodate what is called freedom of expression (as long as it has nothing to do with Christianity). Beyond morality, factual data measuring performance of students in math

Moral truth and belief in God are being mocked in many of the classrooms of our universities.

and science in our country versus other developed countries presents a telling story. We are falling behind. Good, effective leadership is needed everywhere in our education system.

Leadership in Our Government

The world of politics is in chaos. Many people are either from the extreme left or the extreme right. Today our country is engaged in identity politics. People are broken down into groups and subgroups and pitted against one another. Technology is changing the way we communicate and conduct ourselves. The faceless way we can communicate opens up the opportunity to launch vicious attacks against other people. Civil dialogue has gone by the wayside, and the airwaves are saturated with misinformation designed to pit us against one another. Future leaders are needed to navigate through this morass and bring the clarity of morality into the arena of our media, our government, and our politics.

Morality cannot be legislated. It must originate from the hearts and minds of the people. Our Constitution provides the right to choose your religious beliefs, as it should be. Religious beliefs cannot and should not be imposed on people, but as leaders, we can push against immorality and influence the civil discourse. We need courageous men and women who will pursue changes to laws for the good of everyone. Our earlier story of William Wilberforce is a good example of such a person. He started his own crusade to end slavery. Our country needs moral leadership in the political arena that can uphold our Constitution and interpret laws in light of the Constitution.

Today, we are living in an age where the younger generation is witnessing the moral decline of our society and changing values. Generation Z, or the youngest emerging generation, places high value on instant gratification, thinks success is their birthright, and believes that liberal social values are the norm. There are exceptions, but generally speaking, this young generation is not prepared to face the challenges and hardships of life that are sure to come. Much of this is perpetuated by the political ideologies that leaders in the government, media, and education are espousing.

It makes me cringe to listen to our political leaders and pundits in our media (who pass themselves off as intellectual elites) pontificate about social issues when in reality they are moral issues. Religious beliefs are being quashed. If one takes a position on abortion, they are shut down because a court or judge rules and decides that it imposes a religion on others. Having a different point of view is unacceptable if it does not align with those in power. The younger generation is witnessing the labeling of those who stand up for what they believe. People of faith are being labeled as bigots, homophobic, and many other negative labels. Respect for one another is deteriorating. We need strong moral leaders in all areas of our government.

Leadership in the Workplace

Leadership is needed across the entire spectrum of human interaction, but we often think of leadership in the context of the workplace. Most books on leadership focus on business and the impact and influence that leaders make in leading companies to growth and prosperity. Good leadership is crucial if for no other reason than because so many of us are engaged in work of the business enterprise. Many lives are affected by both good and poor leadership, by decisions made and how people are treated.

Business plays a huge role in all of our lives. Business provides work and income to provide for food, shelter, and other needs for our family. Most of us play a role in a business enterprise. Hopefully we find a place where we can thrive. Business leaders know how to build relationships and an environment for growth and development. There is a constant need for leaders and potential leaders in business, and it's a great place to learn, grow, and develop.

The days of working for one organization for a lifetime are gone. The emphasis must be not on lifetime employment but on lifetime employability. That means that change and learning must be a constant, never-ending commitment. Any leader today who wants to thrive has to commit to a lifetime of learning.

Should one choose to be an entrepreneur, the challenges get even more complicated. Again, technology changes almost by the minute, hence a constant need to stay abreast with the latest innovation. Processes are becoming obsolete almost overnight, and then we have to learn how to implement them. If we do not keep up with the changes, we will be left behind. Time and space are shrinking. People expect instant response and can easily move from one supplier to another.

This is not to say technology is all bad. It isn't by a long shot. We can order books from Amazon today and receive them tomorrow. We can find almost anything we want in a matter of seconds on the internet, whether it be services, information, or products. We can use social media and the internet to reach other people all over the world, which was not possible a decade ago. In the midst of all that is happening to speed up the way we get things done, we have less and less discretionary time. We have moved from the physical world to the virtual world and have access to so much at the click of the mouse. I used to research in the library, and I still do from time to time, but I can access information so much faster over the internet. Want some information about any subject? You can ask Google or Siri for general information, but you can also access resources that you can trust as sources for truth. But are we pursuing the things that really matter? We must be discerning!

Leadership of Self

In the midst of our hurried and harassed world, we each have 1,440 minutes every day. How will you invest your 1,440 minutes today? Leadership of self (or discipline) starts with personal choices and self-governance. While we mature as leaders, we must be self-aware of our talents and our time. Counter to our culture, we must ask if our efforts are being directed toward instant gratification and temporal happiness or delayed gratification and long-term success. Better yet, ask yourself, "Are my efforts based on the temporal things or eternal things?" I'll share my answer to this question in the final chapter.

CHAPTER 12

FINAL THOUGHTS

At the very beginning of this book, I acknowledged that I was writing from a Christian worldview. To be more accurate, I should say I am writing from a biblical worldview. There are many worldviews, and everyone has a form of a worldview whether they realize it or not. Our worldview is the lens we use to see the world, which originates from what we know and believe. Our worldview is shaped by our knowledge, beliefs, values, and convictions. What we intrinsically believe guides us in how we see the world, and how we see the world plays out in our behavior. Unfortunately, many have not given deep thought to any particular worldview but more or less have absorbed what they see going on around them and accept whatever they perceive are the cultural norms.

In our current cultural climate, a primary force in the adopted worldview today is based on materialism and secularism. So many lives are guided by what we see and hear as opposed to deep critical thinking. The result is that we fall in line and pursue what the prevailing culture tells us to strive for—going to the right school, getting a stable job, living in a prime location, having fun, and enjoying financial success. These are not bad things, but they don't provide deeper satisfaction. We need to be able to answer such questions like these: Where did I come from? Who am I? Why am I here? Does my life have any meaning beyond the here and now? Why is the world such a broken place?

The secularism and materialism of today's worldview is influenced by the accepted science and what is being taught in our schools. Essentially, they say that life emerged from matter. This matter somehow evolved out of a primordial soupy mass that by chance, over millions of years, became organic and evolved into plant and animal life and eventually our ancient ancestors—all the way to you and me. If this is true, then we are all here by chance or accident.

But if we are here only by chance, then the answers to these questions are really based on opinion, not fact, originating from the mind of human beings evolving over time. The result of this thinking is that truth and our moral underpinnings are whatever the human intellect decides, even to the point of believing that there are no moral absolute truths. At best, morality, right and wrong, is whatever you decide or whatever anyone in power and in control decides. Our days are spent being busy with work, seeking pleasure and temporal things, or pursuing experiences that make us happy. We don't really think about these questions because we are naturally self-focused and live only for what seems to drive us and bring us pleasure and entertainment. Perhaps when we do look for truth, we want it to be something that is easy, painless, and personally satisfying.

What Determines Our Value as a Person?

If we go back to the premise that we evolved from nothing and have come into being by accident, then what is morally right? Who decides what we accept as moral truth? And if we are here by accident, doesn't it make sense that what we accept as truth can change over time and circumstances, with more "enlightenment in each passing generation? If this premise were true, then the moral values of right and wrong and good and evil are subjective and can change depending on circumstances and who has the ultimate power to make that determination. Unfortunately, as we learn more from science, it is used many times as a weapon to degrade the moral beliefs of the Christian worldview. Ironically, our institutions of higher learning, our esteemed universities, were started by those with a Christian worldview, along with many of our hospitals. Frankly, many of these institutions have lost their way.

So, if we are only here by chance, who or what determines our value and worth as a person? A fair question. There are even discussions today about at what point a human being becomes a person. Many believe that a fetus is not a person, and some even claim that a person is not a person until one can reason and be rational and self-conscious. Hence, a baby in the womb has the status of a nonperson and therefore has no rights. And it gets worse! Now, more and more, we hear of infanticide and euthanasia. People of any age, who are deemed incompetent and nonproductive, are reduced to being nonpersons. So, in the guise of compassion, a person's life can be taken because someone can be classified as nonperson, and her life no longer has value. Sounds barbaric, and it is. Sadly, that is the kind of thinking prevalent today.

Sometimes we hear of people facing a lingering death and having time to reflect, and their worldview changes. A rich man who was dying penned the following words:

> I have come to the pinnacle of success in business. In the eyes of others, my life has been the symbol of success. However, apart from work, I have little joy. Finally, my wealth is simply a fact to which I am accustomed. At this time lying on a hospital bed and remembering all my life. I realize that all the accolades and riches of which I was once so proud, have become insignificant with my imminent death. In the dark, when I look at the green lights, of the equipment for artificial respiration and feel the buzz of their mechanical sounds. I can feel the breath of my approaching death looming over me. Only now do I understand that once you accumulate enough money for the rest of your life, you have to pursue objectives that are not related to wealth. It should be something more important. For example, stories of love, art, dreams of my childhood. No, stop pursuing wealth, it can only make a person into a twisted being, just like me.

God has made us one way, we can feel the love in the heart of each of us, and not illusions built by fame or money, like I made in my life. I cannot take them with me, I can only take the memories that were strengthened by love. This is true wealth that will follow you, will accompany you, He will give strength and light to go ahead. Love can travel thousands of miles and so life has no limits. Move to where you want to go. Strive to reach the goals you want to achieve. Everything is in your heart and in your hands. What is the world's most expensive bed? The hospital bed. If you have money you can hire someone to drive your car, but you cannot hire someone to take your illness that is killing you. Material things lost can be found. But one thing you can never find when you lose: life. Whatever stage of life where we are right now, at the end we will have to face the day when the curtain falls. Please treasure your family love, love for your spouse, love for your friends … treat everyone well and stay friendly with your neighbors.

In the end, life is not about material accumulation, fortune, fame, or any other selfish desires. This man's account should make us stop and think about what is lasting and important. It is not the temporal things but the eternal things. My only hope is that this man acknowledged his past sinful nature and placed his faith and trust in Jesus Christ before he breathed his last.

God Created Us

A biblical worldview believes in a universal, sovereign God who is in control and has created everything in our world and the entire universe and whatever is beyond it. Without this belief, nothing else in the biblical or Christian worldview would make any sense. From the beginning of time, God created everything!

The first five words of the Bible set the scene, "In the beginning God created!" This answers the question, "Where did I come from?" The narrative in Genesis and throughout the Bible makes it clear that God is the creator of all things, seen and unseen, and is behind the intelligent design of our world and our universe. At the very pinnacle of God's creation is man and woman, who were created in His image. From that standing, every human being from the time of conception until death has a high value. The worldview of a Christian is that life is sacred and precious. Therefore, no matter what state of mind or season in life, or how developed in the womb, a human being created in the image of God is valuable and has a purpose. There are no nonpersons. A person with a Christian worldview must place a high value on all human life regardless of whether they have the same beliefs or not!

At first, the entire creation was all very good—until humankind's fall, when sin entered into the world. As a result, God punished Adam and Eve by banishing them from the garden and allowed hardship and death and decay to happen to every living thing. Looking as far back as we want, the ultimate earthly destination for all of us is death. The statistics are overwhelmingly conclusive. Rich and poor, privileged and powerful, young and old, we all succumb to our ultimate end, at least in the physical realm. In the end, all the gain we might have accumulated, all the acclaim we may have received for our accomplishments, and all the entertainment we have consumed will mean absolutely nothing.

In the context of God's common grace, it is important to always remember that God has gifted us all with talent.

God Is Holy

The biblical worldview believes that God is holy. This quality is all about His purity and perfection. This poses a problem for all of us. We are far from pure and perfect. Not even close. God cannot accept us as we are with our rebellious and self-centered nature. It is not possible for His nature to be at one with our nature; hence we have a broken and fractured relationship with the Creator who made us. The Bible is clear about our original state. It says, "But your iniquities have made a separation from between you and your God and your sins have hidden his face from you so that he does not hear" (Isaiah 59:2). When and if we get to the point where we see ourselves as sinful beings, we will begin to understand the question, "Who am I?"

God Is Just

God is righteous, fair, and good—and we are not! God must act in conformity to who He is. He will judge us all in accordance with what is merited or deserved. He is exact and precise in His judgment. If we remain in a state of rebellion and live out our sinful nature, we will face a severe judgment for all eternity. There will be no place to hide or mask who we are. Adding to the problem, no one will ever be good enough to meet God's standards. In other words, we are all equally lost and on our own cannot meet God's standards of holiness! But there is a way for us to escape God's pending punishment.

God Is Loving

Many have memorized John 3:16, which states, "For God so loved the world, that he gave his only Son, that whoever believes in him shall not perish but have eternal life." The following verse is also important, "For God did not send his Son into the to condemn the world, but in order that world might be saved through him" (John 3:17).

The central theme throughout the Bible is God's redemptive plan for our salvation from His wrath. All of us will face it if we choose not to confess and repent and place our trust and faith in the one God sent to pay the debt of our sin, Jesus Christ. Jesus is God. While Mary was Jesus's earthly mother, He was conceived by the Holy Spirit. So Jesus was fully human, as He had human limitations, but also fully God, and He lived a perfectly holy and righteous life. It is a historical fact that Jesus was crucified and died a cruel death on a cross, willingly sacrificing His life to pay for the sins of all of us. Jesus lived and died as our substitute. Many people know the story. Jesus was crucified, He died, and when He died, God exercised His judgment against all sins of those who are lost and living sinful lives.

Jesus died to pay the penalty for our sin. We must, however, respond by repenting of our sin and placing our trust and faith in Jesus Christ as our Lord and Savior. It means turning our life over to being a Christ follower in the here and now. It means that we will grow and learn to be obedient to the truth of the Gospel, believing that through God's power and because of our personal relationship with Jesus, we now have what we need to live a life not governed by sin.

What Happens When We Believe?

When we believe and are willing to follow God, our spirits will be reconnected to our Creator. Being a Christ follower is not easy. For one, He wants to change us radically from the inside out. Second, many will scoff at the whole idea of our conversion, and we may face some ridicule. In other countries, it is truly a life-threatening decision. In fact, more people are martyred today for standing up for their Christian faith than any other time in history. When we make the decision to be a Christ follower, our worldview changes. We get clarity about who we are (adopted into the family of God), why we are here (to serve and bring glory to God), and where we are going (ultimately to live in the presence of God in heaven). We will know that our life has meaning beyond the here and now (to be with God forever), and finally, we will understand why our world is such a broken place (because of our sinful nature).

How Then Shall We Lead?

How does this truth about God and the world affect the leader? When God created us in His image, He blessed us with natural talent themes, an ability to be self-aware, a conscience, and a free will to make choices. What God has given to all humankind is His common grace, which is His unmerited goodness toward all of us even though we do not deserve it and cannot earn it. God cares for His creation and uses all people to nurture the world. In the context of God's common grace, it is important to always remember that God has gifted us all with talent. If a person refuses to follow Christ, it does not mean they will be deprived of talent to make a contribution for good. There are people I trust and admire who do not believe as I do, but they are more talented and more competent to perform a task or assignment than I am. If you are a leader with a Christian worldview, we must respect and love the people we lead and acknowledge their contributions, whether or not they are fellow believers. We are commanded to love everyone, and that includes our enemies or those we dislike.

We should not lose sight of the fact that God provides for His people through the work of others. My mechanic can fix my car because he has the knowledge, skills, and expertise that I lack. We should not be taken by surprise that people who are not Christians can do great work! Many times better than Christians! God providentially takes care of His creation by using all kinds of people. If you are a Christian leader, you should continue to place a high value on the work done by others, in particular those whose work exemplifies excellence, regardless of where they go to church. We should share what we believe but not be judgmental. We should follow the advice of Peter when he said this in 1 Peter 3:15:

> But in your hearts honor Christ the Lord as holy, always being prepared to make a defense to anyone who asks you for a reason for the hope that is in you; yet do it with gentleness and respect.

A Christian leader is motivated by moral convictions that inspires her to honor God and serve with excellence, honesty, and integrity while caring for those whom she leads. Also, the Christian leader must be aware that there are many who approach their lives with honesty, integrity, a sense of justice, and a desire to do right for others, even though they may not have experienced the saving grace of Christ. All of us are born with a conscience and a sense of right and wrong. Romans 2:15 points out this:

> They show that the work of the law is written on their hearts, while their conscience also bears witness and their conflicting thoughts accuse them or even excuse them.

God, from the beginning, has wired us up with a sense of knowing right and wrong. There are people who act like they're upholding biblical principles even though they are not professing Christians. We can respect leaders who have a strong character, who are competent, who have convictions, and who display courage even though the motivation of the heart may not be centered on bringing glory to God.

The World Needs You

May all who read this lead and serve to inspire, influence, and make an impact. May you be encouraged to leave a legacy focused on hope that will live beyond the temporal. The world desperately needs leaders who place high emphasis on character and commit to hold themselves accountable to be trustworthy, authentic, compelling, courageous, persevering, and humble enough to see themselves as servants. Jesus, while speaking to the disciples after they argued who was the greatest, put it bluntly, "If anyone would be first, he must be last of all and servant of all" (Mark 9:35).

Leaders might not be out in front, but they will always have a big responsibility to bring out the best in those who follow them. A good leader doesn't lord over people but instead serves them—not by treating them harshly but by inspiring them with his character, competence, conviction, and courage.

Leadership truly matters. Leader, the power to make positive change is in your hands.

ABOUT THE AUTHOR

Bob Johnson held senior leadership positions in three companies over the course of thirty-seven years, and later launched a consulting company that provides coaching services to organizations. He has served on multiple boards and has also been an active member of the Christian Business Men's Committee. Bob and his wife, Barbara, reside in Trabuco Canyon, California.